PROMISES
to KEEP

PROMISES to KEEP

The Untold Story of a Family

Trapped in War-Torn Italy

by

Thomas F. Dwyer, Ed. D

iUniverse, Inc.
New York   Bloomington

iUniverse books may be ordered through booksellers or by contacting:

iUniverse
1663 Liberty Drive
Bloomington, IN 47403
www.iuniverse.com
1-800-Authors (1-800-288-4677)

ISBN: 978-0-595-52900-1 (sc)
ISBN: 978-0-595-62950-3 (ebook)
ISBN: 978-0-595-51871-5 (dj)

Printed in the United States of America

iUniverse rev. date: 5/18/2009

To Maria

Contents

ACKNOWLEDGMENTS

I wish to thank the surviving members of the Forte family for letting this story be told. I am certain that many readers will share in my gratitude.

Thanks also to Don Kaiser for sharing his insightful Web site at http://www.warwingsart.com12thairforce//vesuvius.html with me. Don's father, Technical Sgt. Quentin C. Kaiser, a radioman/waist gunner with sixty-five missions under his belt, also has a Web site, http://www.warwingsart.com/12thairforce/page.html. Together they offer a compelling pictorial and anecdotal insight into the air war in the Mediterranean.

I would be remiss if I failed to acknowledge the fine editorial oversight provided by Lillian Quinn. She managed somehow to successfully reign in my enthusiastic attempts to push the English language in directions it was not intended to go.

I also wish to thank United Press International, Beacon Press, Random House and Donadio & Olson for generously allowing me to reproduce their copyrighted materials.

Finally, I want to recognize the timely and professional efforts of the research staffs at both the National Archives & Records Administration in College Park, Maryland, and the Army Heritage and Educational Center in Carlisle, Pennsylvania. The photographs that they unearthed were central to the preparation of this book.

INTRODUCTION

Several hundred years ago, the renaissance humanist Desiderius Erasmus noted, "War is delightful to those who have had no experience of it." Indeed, war is the ultimate obscenity. It is hardly surprising, therefore, that it, in turn, breeds obscenity. The Rape of Nanking, the Bataan Death March, the annihilation of Lidice, and the massacre at My Lai all stand out as grim reminders of man's capacity for brutality. The tiny village of Pico was also such a place. A mere dot on the Italian provincial map of Frosinone, it consists of slightly more than three thousand souls, living in a thirty-two-square-kilometer area, midway between Rome and Naples. Its global positioning coordinates are forty-one degrees, twenty-seven minutes north, and thirteen degrees, thirty-three minutes east. Although this is interesting and important information, it tells us nothing about the people of Pico or the reasons behind its fleeting military importance during World War II.

Pico was arguably one of the most peaceful places on Earth. Located in the gently rolling foothills of the Aurunci Mountains in Central Italy, it was nestled part way up the side of a hill, as though its medieval builders thought better than to lug mortar and stone all the way to the top. Its narrow cobblestone streets, burnished to a gloss by centuries of wear and marked by an occasional shop or bistro, twist up and down the lazy incline, binding the whole thing together. It was also home to three churches (four if you count the one in the cemetery) along with the obligatory remains of a once proud feudal castle. In the center of what served as the village square, a large tree offered an island of shade from the blistering Italian sun. Life in the tiny *paese* was conducted at a casual pace, and, accordingly, in early afternoon, all social and commercial activity ceased while its citizens surrendered to the welcome lure of *siesta*. As if it were possible, the outskirts of town were even more sedate. Sheep and goats grazed without restraint in the shadow of the slumbering foothills, their hindquarters marked with a dab of paint that, should they wander off, guaranteed their prompt return to their owners.

Whatever its pastoral serenity, Pico was surrounded by the remnants of a long history of conquest. A short distance to the north lay the Eternal City of Rome, still firmly in the grip of German occupation forces. In 1944, it was also the only Axis capital in danger of falling, and its capture would be of great propaganda value. To the northeast lay the centuries-old Adriatic seaport of Pescara. Once a major trading port for the eastern provinces of the Roman Empire, it had been reduced to rubble, the victim of repeated Allied air attacks. To the west lay the ancient Appian Way, stretching from Rome to Brindisi, at the heel of the Italian boot. A classic model of civil engineering, it had served as the preferred line of march from Caesar to Napoleon. By the spring of 1944, it marked the path of German troop movements as they moved along the Tyrrhenian Coast.

Finally, to the south, lay the city of Foggia. Once the thirteenth-century palatial retreat of Fredrick II, it had become the twentieth-century headquarters for two hundred medium and heavy bombers, which, laden with over four hundred tons of explosives, were taxiing into position throughout the region. Their mission would set in motion a chain of events that would change the lives of the Picanos forever.

* * *

Ironically, it was the very nature of the formidable Aurunci Mountains that would turn them into instruments of war. Their towering presence, along with a labyrinth of strong rivers, would provide the setting for some of the most brutal combat of World War II. Although fighting had been fierce throughout the entire Italian Campaign, the worst occurred along what was to become known as the Gustav Line: a powerful complex of German defensive positions strung across the entire width of the central Italian peninsula. Put together under the command of Field Marshal Albert Kesselring, its sole purpose was to slow the relentless surge of Allied forces up the Italian boot.

Born in Bavaria, the son of a schoolmaster, Kesselring served as an artillery lieutenant in the First World War. At age sixty-three, and fiercely loyal to Hitler, he had been given command of all German armed forces in Italy and was making his enemies pay dearly for every inch of ground. In early 1944, the Allied armies, finding themselves stalled along the Gustav Line, launched a series of attacks against the German defenders in and around the town of Cassino and its nearby mountaintop abbey. The synchronized plan included a daring amphibious landing behind the German lines at the coastal town of Anzio. Once known as Antium, Anzio was, in fact, older than Rome itself. Along with Terracina to its south, it was a favorite resort of the ancients. It was also the birthplace of two of the worst tyrants in Roman history: Nero and Caligula.

Located roughly thirty miles south of Rome, Anzio was bounded on the south by over one hundred and seventy-five thousand acres of wetlands known as the Pontine Marshes. These wetlands were long notorious as a malarial breeding ground. In the early twentieth century, Mussolini ordered that a massive project be undertaken to reclaim these wetlands. An extensive canal system was then installed, along with strategically placed pumping stations. The elaborate drainage system worked well, and the marsh was successfully transformed into rich, tillable farmland.

In early 1944, the Allied landing was expected to serve two purposes: first, it would undermine the Gustav Line from the rear; and second, it would threaten the German occupation of Rome. The landing was perfectly designed and flawlessly executed. Kesselring was caught completely by surprise, and on January 22, the more than forty thousand American and British troops who stormed ashore practically unopposed under the command of U.S. General

John Lucas, now stood poised to break the back of the German defenses.

This decisive tactical coup would quickly evaporate into a massive strategic disaster. The American commander took several days to consolidate the beachhead and was unable to exploit his advantage of surprise. This delay gave Kesselring more than enough time to recover.

Lucas's problems were further compounded by the fact that Kesselring's engineers were able to destroy Mussolini's canals and pumping stations, thus returning the Pontine Marshes to a vast swampland. Their action essentially crippled Lucas's right flank and enabled Kesselring to focus his firepower along the rest of the line. Within days, German tanks and artillery surrounded the Allied foothold and proceeded to pour shells, at will, into the tiny beachhead. Although Anzio lay a mere sixty miles behind the Gustav Line, it may as well have been six hundred. In an attempt to take advantage of the diversion of German troops to Anzio, the Allies immediately launched a second direct frontal attack in the Cassino area. The battle soon ground to a bloody halt, and the town of Cassino, which served as the fulcrum of the Gustav Line, was still doggedly held by German Grenadiers who had been ordered by Hitler to stand or die.

Then there was the abbey itself. Founded by Saint Benedict in the sixth century, it was one of the most famous monasteries in all of Christendom. It had also been plagued by a long and unfortunate history. It was first destroyed by the Lombards during the sixth century and was rebuilt, only to be destroyed again by ninth century Saracen hoards. Rebuilt for the third time, it was once again reduced to ruins in 1349 by an earthquake. By 1944, the extensively restored abbey served as the home of many priceless artworks as well as the final resting place for several Christian saints, including Saint Benedict and his sister, Saint Scholastica.

Ensconced high atop Monte Cassino, the abbey offered a sweeping view of the entire valley in which Allied soldiers were being cut down by German artillery fire. It was reasoned that the monastery's command of the high ground immediately behind the town of Cassino made it extremely valuable, as both a German defensive fortress and as an observation platform from which to rain destruction into the valley below. Like their comrades at Anzio, the Allied troops in the valley were now trapped and at the mercy of German artillery.

At this point, it was decided to once again assault both the mountain and the town, and an air attack was planned to soften the German positions in the abbey. The Allied command had no way of knowing it, of course, but the only German soldier to enter the abbey was the commander of the defending German paratroops, General Frido von Senger und Etterlin, and only on those occasions when he might attend Mass in the crypt. Nor were they aware that the German general was also a lay member of the Benedictine order and had expressly forbid any German military occupation of the monastery. He had even gone so far as to post guards to ensure that his order was carried out. The existing natural terrain atop the mountain was more than adequate for his purposes. Under considerable pressure from Churchill to break the stalemate, the Allied high command eventually gave the order to bomb the abbey as soon as weather permitted.

It has been said that truth is often the first casualty of war. The story that you are about to read is an attempt to fill that void. It chronicles the happenings at Pico from two different perspectives. On the larger level, it examines the military backdrop against which the taking of Pico occurred, as well as the military celebrities in command when it all happened. This is a matter of well-documented history, an effort greatly aided by the readings listed at the end of this book. On a more personal level, this story also deals with the lives of some of the people caught up in that conflagration. Their family name is Forte, and the stories that unfold herein have been an extension of their oral family history for more than half a century. These events did happen, and although I have taken some minor creative license by structuring dialogue and framing events, this narrative remains faithful to its anecdotal evidence. I have also changed the names of some of the peripheral characters for the sake of their privacy.

I would caution the reader that this is not a pretty story. It is impossible to describe war delicately; nevertheless, nothing in this book has been included merely for dramatic effect. The events contained herein, no matter how troubling, actually occurred. These are real events that happened to real people, in an almost unreal setting. If it also makes us ponder the foreboding possibility that war might someday scorch its path down the main streets of our hometowns, then it will have served its purpose.

Tom Dwyer

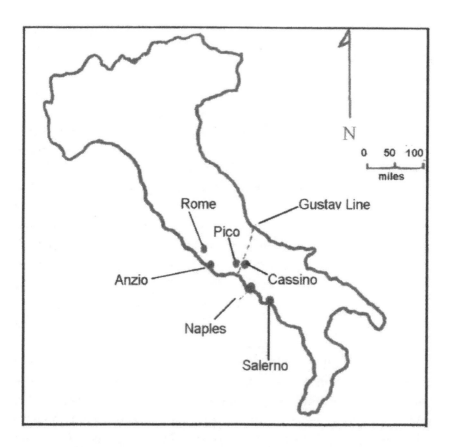

The Italian Campaign stalled along the Gustav Line in early 1944.

CHAPTER ONE
The Beginning of the End

We make this wide encircling movement in the Mediterranean, having for its primary object the recovery of command of that vital sea, but also having for its object the exposure of the underbelly of the Axis, especially Italy, to heavy attack.

—Winston Churchill, November 11, 1942

It was shortly after 9:00 AM on Tuesday, February 15, when eight-year-old Maria Forte, along with her little dog and her best friend, Sabetta, walked briskly through the chill that hung in the morning air on the tiny Italian farm. Friends for as long as either could remember, they went to school together, spent most of their waking hours together, and on days like today, even did chores together. The dog was a small mongrel of unknown ancestry, a friendly thing, with large black spots and an absurd orange blotch across the nape of his neck. As a young farm girl, Maria had learned not to adopt any of the animals as pets. Her little mixed breed was the one exception to this rule; in spite of this special status, however, he was simply known as Dog.

Pushed by shifting winds, the stench of gun powder from yesterday's artillery duel now permeated the foothills around Pico. A scattering of small blue patches filtered through the clouds, suggesting that the long, dismal rainy season might be over. This winter had even brought some snow. It was a stingy snow that neither accumulated nor lasted. When it did fall, however, the two girls would scamper about, scoop the snow into cups, and sprinkle them with a few drops of wine. Once the treats were devoured, they rinsed their cups and prayed for more snow. As they neared the henhouse, the chickens began milling about nervously while the resident rooster craned his neck and flared his wings in protest of this unwelcome trespass into his harem. As if mocking his fuss, Maria cupped her hand behind her ear. "Listen, Sabetta! Do you hear that?"

"How could I *not* hear it?" her friend frowned. "Anyhow, it's just the same old noise he always makes."

"No, no, besides him, I mean. There isn't any more thunder this morning."

"You're right!" Sabetta's eyes widened as she turned toward where the mountains cascaded southward. "Do you suppose it means the fighting has stopped?"

For over a month, the village of Pico had woken daily to the sounds of war, roughly ten miles away. Maria had heard the adults speak often about a great battle being fought in nearby Cassino, and that once it was over, the victorious Americans would, no doubt, be coming to their village. Now that the noise had stopped, perhaps it meant that the Americans would be here soon. That would be a good thing, because her father, Domenico Forte, was living in America, and she wanted very much to go there and meet him for the first time.

Comforted by the silence beyond the horizon, Maria and Sabetta continued on toward the henhouse, fanning seed, while the chickens dashed about, forming tiny scrums at each dropping of grain. As they walked along, Maria reflected on the significance of her job; after all, chickens were very important to life on the farm. First, of course, there were the eggs. The math was simple, one day, one chicken, one egg. There were eighteen chickens, so that meant eighteen eggs each day. There were nine mouths to feed: Maria; her mother, Maria Civita; her two brothers, Rosario and Attilio; her sister-in-law, Vittoria; her nephew, Mimino; her aunt, Menica; and her two grandparents. It didn't always come out perfect. Sometimes two or three chickens would forget, but on a good day, each person was treated to two eggs.

Maria's thoughts were suddenly jolted back to the henhouse by the sight of the struggling hen whose eyes bulged like marbles as she strained in a futile attempt to deposit her egg.

"Look at the poor thing," she said.

2

"Is there something we can do?" asked Sabetta.

"I'm not sure, but maybe if I ..."

Maria reached down and lifted the hen from the nest, gently grabbed the partially emerged egg with her fingers, and tugged on it slightly. With that, the egg popped out and the hen suddenly cackled, as if in relief.

"There," said Maria, returning the hen to its roost. "That's better now; isn't it?"

She then placed the egg in Sabetta's upraised apron and the two girls proceeded to rummage through the rest of the hen house.

"That's it for in here," said Sabetta. "Now let's look in the haystack."

The girls exchanged knowing nods. Very often, some hens would climb onto the perimeter of the haystack, burnish little pockets with their torsos, and proceed to lay their eggs. This is where Dog became an important member of the egg-fetching team. Upon seeing the girls move toward the haystack, he would instinctively rush ahead and sniff out the spot where a hen was nesting. Ignoring her protest, he would push her aside with his nose, pick up the egg with his teeth, return to Maria, and gently deposit it into her outstretched hand. The egg-napper would then repeat the process for as long as any eggs remained in the haystack. Dog had been doing this for as long as Maria could remember, and he was so accomplished at the task, she thought it to be a universal canine skill.

Soon Sabetta's apron was filled with the harvest, but as the girls turned to walk back toward the house, they heard an unfamiliar rumble coming from behind the southern horizon. Suddenly, the sky was filled with warplanes, and bomb after bomb began crashing into the monastery atop Monte Cassino. Hens scattered wildly about as the girls staggered back against the henhouse wall. Huge columns of smoke spit skyward from atop the mountain. The henhouse wall began to shake, causing Sabetta to release her grip on her apron. Eighteen eggs also fell, crashing to the ground. High above their heads, the giant formation curled into a sweeping arc as the children ran screaming toward the farmhouse.

* * *

Even by New England standards, it was cold—so cold that the fresh-fallen snow crunched beneath his boots as fifty-three-year-old Domenico Forte stepped down from the bus and out into the night. Short, with powerful arms hanging from his stocky frame, he was a jolly sort and generous to a fault. His wardrobe consisted entirely of work clothes, high-cut shoes, and, if one included accessories, a lunch pail. Startled by the sudden icy sting on his neck, he flipped his buttonless collar up around his neck, gripped the front firmly with one hand, and began the mile-long trek to his two-room apartment. It had snowed throughout the day, and since no one had as yet shoveled their walks, he plodded home through the narrow tire tracks in the roadway with the mechanical cadence of a wind-up toy. Although he had never acquired a taste for winters in the Berkshires, during the twenty-one years he spent wandering across the United States, he would always return to these gently rolling hills because they reminded him of the Aurunci Mountain foothills that surrounded his family's farm in Pico.

Immensely proud to have voted in the last two elections, he nevertheless paid little attention to such things as international tension or the German invasion of Poland. These matters were better left to those who understood them—until now! News reports of military events suddenly changed all of that, inasmuch as his family in Pico might well be in danger. Throughout the winter, reports from the front told of a bloody line of battle that had slowly migrated up the Italian peninsula and presently raged a mere ten miles from his family's farm. Aside from idle gossip from his second shift co-workers that "something was happening," most news reports were predicting that there would soon be another major assault against the German lines, and if that were so, he knew that no good could possibly come of it.

When he reached his Columbus Avenue apartment, Domenico paused for a moment to study the Parker house, which stood directly across the street. Nice lady, Mrs. Parker, always waving and chatting. Last summer, her son Jake joined the Marine Corps right out of high school. It happened last Thanksgiving on a small island that Domenico had never heard of, called Tarawa. In one of the most savage battles of the Pacific war, over three thousand marines, including young Jake

4

Parker, were killed. Things were much different now. Mrs. Parker had become a recluse, hiding from the outside world behind forever-drawn shades. In her front window hung a small, rectangular, red-bordered cloth, fringed with yellow tassels and centered by a small gold star, silently proclaiming to all who passed that young Jake Parker would never be coming home.

Domenico shook his head and turned up the walkway to his apartment. He stomped the snow from his shoes, unlocked the door, and fumbled for the entry foyer light. At last, able to feel his toes and see what he was doing, he picked up the remnants of a newspaper and labored up the stairs to his tiny apartment. As was his custom, his landlord, Mr. Balducci, had left the newspaper for Domenico—an act for which he was sincerely grateful. On the other hand, Mrs. Balducci would systematically disembowel the newspaper and refold it in a way that one would wrap fish parts. For this, Domenico was not so grateful. He tossed the paper, such as it was, onto the small linoleum-topped table in the kitchenette, rinsed out his thermos, and lifted an old, thickly caked pipe from his coat pocket. With pipe in hand, he then retrieved a small box of cigars from the drain board. They resembled charcoal twigs more than they did tobacco. He broke one of them into small pieces and pressed the resultant mess into the bowl of his pipe with the stub that was once the middle finger of his right hand. He looked forward to the sharp bite that the tobacco would soon deliver. In truth, he had long since become indifferent to the unkind remarks made about its wretched odor.

Whenever he tamped his tobacco with the one-knuckled finger, his thoughts would return to that day in the factory when he made the fateful mistake. It was the duty of a crane hitcher to see that the large steel cables were properly secured to whatever object was being lifted, and once satisfied that the load was in balance, to slide the cables onto the lifting crane's giant hook. He remembered hitching the load and circling the raised index finger of his left hand, signaling the crane operator that the load was ready to be lifted. In a moment that he would regret for the rest of his life, Domenico forgot that he still had the middle finger of his right hand around the cable. It took only a fraction of a second before the one-inch-thick steel cable pulled taught against the giant hook and the upper half of his finger fell to the factory floor. Now, as he sat at the table staring down at his painfully acquired tamping tool, he thought aloud, "Stubido!"

He picked up his newspaper and turned to the first section. It showed an item that had been circled in the evening's listing of radio programs. It was one of his landlord's favorites: Gabriel Heatter at 9:00 PM. Domenico had listened to the program a few times and thought this Heatter fellow to be rather odd. Here it was, 1944, with the world self-destructing all around him, and Heatter would religiously begin every broadcast with the words, "There's good news tonight." He made a silent prayer that for tonight, at least, Heatter was right.

At last—the front page! Slowly and deliberately, the words of his newly adopted language formed on his lips as he read the headlines.

> *Allied Headquarters, Naples, (UP) - American Flying Fortresses and big siege guns of the Fifth Army poured a drumfire of death into the ancient Benedictine monastery of Monte Cassino today, and front reports said the two-way bombardment had knocked out the powerful German defenses inside the shrine and on the surrounding mountain slopes.*[1]

No! This can't be! The newspaper crumbled in his fists. The unlit pipe fell to the floor. His face slumped forward into the paper. *"Padre eterno! Che so fatto?"* He moaned between sobs, "Eternal Father! What have I done?"

---

[1] Copyright © United Press International, February 15, 1944. Reprinted by permission of UPI.

National Archives and Records Administration
February 7, 1944: Allied artillery pummels Castle Hill in the town of Cassino, directly below the abbey.

National Archives and Records Administration
February 15, 1944: The destruction of the Benedictine abbey.

CHAPTER TWO
A Promise Delayed: 1910–14

Give me your tired, your poor,
Your huddled masses yearning to breathe free,
The wretched refuse of your teeming shore.
Send these, the homeless, tempest-tossed to me,
I lift my lamp beside the golden door!

—Emma Lazarus, "The New Colossus," 1883

It was in the early spring of 1910. The Italian sun bore down on young Domenico Forte as he guided the plow silently through the rich topsoil of his family's hillside farm. As he reached the end of each row, he reflexively reined in the horse and wrestled the plow into a half circle. After each turn, he stopped and wiped his forearm across the sweat that burned his eyes. The sweat from his arm just made them burn worse. It was enough for one day. Haunted by the certainty that the plow would still be waiting for them in the morning, he released the harness and led the horse back toward the barn.

As a young man, Domenico understood nothing beyond the drudgery of life on the small farm where he lived with his parents and two sisters. There were fields to be plowed, harvests to bring in, and animals to be fed. It was a hard life, but better, he reasoned, than most of the families nearby, who were, in large part, poor sharecroppers. For them, the land took everything and gave back only a fraction of its yield. At eighteen years of age, he had already grown skeptical of life as he knew it in the little wood plank house, bleached by the sun and worn by the years.

On this day, however, a letter arrived. It was from his cousin living in a town named Beverly, in a strange-sounding state somewhere in America. It told of the good life there and the promise of fine wages in a shoe factory where most of the people in the town were employed. That was all he needed to know. Once the crop was in the ground, he was bound for Naples, where, working for his passage, he would sail off to the promise of the shoe factory.

The town of Beverly is located on the northeast shore of Massachusetts Bay, about twenty miles from Boston. True to his cousin's word, Domenico found a large Italian community, many of whom worked in the shoe factory. Unfortunately, at the time of his arrival, there were no job openings, and since he seriously lacked occupational and language skills, he quickly discovered that he was otherwise unemployable. Through the local grapevine, however, he learned of a job working on a large truck farm in nearby Southern Maine. Tempted by the opportunity, he journeyed north and was promptly put to work plowing fields, cleaning stables, milking cows, and slopping pigs—precisely the tasks from which he had hoped to escape. To make matters worse, he was given little, if any, pay, fed once a day, and forced to sleep in a barn with the farm animals. Three months had gone by, and he still owned nothing more than the shirt on his back. Late summer found him riding the rails back to Beverly, where he managed to pick up occasional work as a day laborer. Unfortunately, his visa was about to expire, so using his meager savings, he purchased train fare back to New York City, where he secured another work-for-passage arrangement for his return to Pico.

Shortly after returning to Italy, he fell in love with fifteen-year-old Maria Civita DiMugno. They had first met in town, where her parents ran a small shop. It was casual at first, no more than a light flirtation. Domenico soon found excuses go into town more often, and he quickly became her Romeo and she, his Juliet. Things started going badly, however, when her parents learned of their relationship. Maria came from a family of moderately successful merchants while Domenico's austere farming background promised nothing. In spite of her parents' objections, the young lovers continued to meet secretly. A few months later, her father learned from a customer that they were still seeing one another and confronted Maria Civita with the news.

"He yelled like a madman," she told Domenico.

"What's he going to do?" he asked.

"He said that as soon as he can make arrangements, he is going to bring me to a convent in Frosinone. I believe he means it."

"What can we do to stop him?"

"Tell him the truth, I guess."

"Tell him what truth?" asked the puzzled Domenico.

"That we are going to have a child!"

They were married in Pico, at the Church of Sant' Antonio in October 1913.

With a bride in hand and a child soon to come, Domenico became painfully aware that although his family responsibilities had increased dramatically, his economic prospects had not. For the next few months, he continued to struggle with the land. It only reinforced his belief that if he remained in Pico, in all likelihood, he would die exactly as he came into this world: a poor dirt farmer. The choice was simple; he would return to America as soon as possible. His plan, like many Italian husbands of the day, was to cash in on any opportunity that presented itself and return with whatever he could save. During his earlier trip to Beverly, he learned of a city at the other end of the state called Pittsfield. It was the home of General Electric, a large electrical manufacturing firm, which employed over ten thousand people. Better yet, it was said to be home to a large number of Italian immigrants, some of whom even came from Pico. Buoyed by this new promise, he decided that America had not seen the last of him. There was little time to waste. On March 7, 1914, twenty-three-year-old Domenico Forte once again set sail for the United States, this time aboard the aptly named *S.S. America*. Three days after he sailed, Maria Civita gave birth to their first son, Angelo.

Domenico's situation in Pittsfield proved to be far more rewarding than his earlier experience in Beverly. Life among the Italian immigrants on the east side of town was perfect, given his circumstances. Hampered by a serious language barrier, many Italians new to the country tended to congregate in small communities. They spoke primarily Italian, attended ethnic churches, shopped in Italian-speaking stores, and read *El Progresso*. This was true in most of the factory towns that dotted the northeast, but because of their nearness to immigration entry ports, it was particularly prevalent in New York, Massachusetts, and Rhode Island.

Factory work was hard, and the hours were long, but within a year, Domenico had saved a few dollars, which he would bring back to the farm along with the certainty that a better life was still possible. He thanked God daily that he had been able to drive a stake into the ground at last! However, things would soon turn sour. The newspaper headlines on that fateful day in June 1914 proclaimed how, in Sarajevo, a young Bosnian student named Gavrilo Princip, living in Serbia, jumped onto the running board of a car carrying Archduke Ferdinand and his wife Sophia and shot them both. The archduke was heir to the thrones of both Austria and Hungary, and his assassination instantly triggered a series of diplomatic crises. Within a month, the Austro-Hungarian Empire demanded that Serbia allow them to have a say in the trial of the archduke's assassin. Serbia promptly dismissed the ultimatum, and on July 28, 1914, Austria-Hungary declared war on Serbia. A convoluted series of events quickly followed. Within a week, Austria's ally, Germany, declared war on Russia and France and then immediately began marching through Belgium. The madness then spread to Turkey, Romania, and Great Britain, thereby lighting the torch of World War I.

Back in Italy, there was considerable disagreement over Italian participation in the war, and, as a result, Italy did not immediately become involved. Concerned by reports that Italy was teetering on the brink of war, young Domenico hurried home to his family. Although his great American dream was once again on hold, he would at least be able to see his one-year-old son, Angelo, for the first time.

A few hundred miles to the north of the route Domenico's ship had taken, a German U-boat torpedoed and sunk the British passenger liner *Lusitania* just off the coast of Ireland. Over twelve hundred civilian passengers lost their lives, including one hundred and twenty-eight Americans. This disaster would eventually tip the scales for the otherwise neutral United States to enter the war against Germany.

In a remotely related matter, thirty-one-year-old firebrand Benito Mussolini was dismissed from the Italian Socialist Party because of his strong pro-war position. Not easily silenced, he then founded a newspaper in Forli called *Il Papolo d' Italia* and immediately began to use it as an editorial platform to persuade Italy to enter the war as soon as possible. Mussolini would get his wish. By May 1915, events had deteriorated to the point that the Italian government declared war on Austria-Hungary and marched immediately into southern Austria. The assassination of the archduke had now become known as the "shot heard around the world."

A simple man, Domenico knew little about the archduke's importance and even less about the international repercussions of his murder; nevertheless, he soon found himself conscripted into the Italian infantry as a machine gunner. With a crop in the field and a wife and child at home, the reluctant patriot would spend the next two years fighting in an endless series of indecisive battles in the north of Italy, along the Austrian border. As it did on the western front, the fighting in Italy eventually settled into stagnant, bloody trench warfare. Life in the rugged mountain terrain would become the central topic of Domenico's long letters home. His only comfort came from the knowledge that life in the enemy trenches was just as miserable as his.

After suffering disastrous losses in the fall of 1917, the Italian high command became wary of initiating any major action for the better part of a year. This "do nothing" strategy was unacceptable to the Allies, so General Armando Diaz, the newly appointed Italian chief of staff, promptly sent fifty-seven divisions into battle across the Piave River in an attempt to cut off the Austro-Hungarian supply lines that ran through the town of Vittorio Veneto.

As fate would have it, Domenico and his ammunition carrier, Patsy, occupied a forward trench in the division that was to spearhead this drive. Although they had been together since infantry training, Domenico and Patsy were a classic example of opposites attracting. Survival in the trenches of World War I was problematic at best, and it was this danger that fueled their camaraderie. Separately, each had been shaped by hard work and poverty, but together, they derived strength from the commonality of those experiences. Like many soldiers in many wars, they spoke longingly of home and loved ones. Domenico often retraced his experiences in America for Patsy, and together they vowed to go there, if and when this wretched war would ever end.

For his part, Patsy was a rough and tumble product of the streets of Naples, whose black handlebar moustache hid the impish grin of a chronic prankster. On the other hand, Domenico's trusting, rural manner usually found him on the receiving end of many of Patsy's tricks. Shortly after they were assigned to a forward trench, Patsy called Domenico aside and seriously intoned, "I just heard the captain is looking for volunteers."

"I never volunteer for anything," answered Domenico.

"Well, you might want to reconsider. This time it's for some special retrieval project back at cavalry headquarters."

"Headquarters, you say?"

"Yeah. It sounds like a good way to get out of this lousy trench for a few hours."

"That makes sense, Patsy. I'll do it. Thanks!"

Cavalry headquarters turned out to be a large horse paddock where Domenico spent the day "retrieving" horse droppings. He would reward Patsy for this kindness by lacing his canteen with vinegar.

It was early on the morning of October 23 when they first heard the roar of Italian artillery from their rear as it began softening the enemy positions on the other side of no-man's-land. "This must be what the captain meant when he said a *big one* was coming," said Patsy. Domenico, his attention locked onto the whining shells as they passed overhead, nodded in silent agreement. The Battle of Vittorio Veneto was about to begin.

Carefully, the two men inched their way up the walls of the slit trench and peered out over the edge, only to discover that the artillery shells were landing at least seventy yards short of the enemy positions. With their attention fixed on the thunderous fusillade, neither man heard the captain slip into the trench behind them.

"Are you two crazy?" he barked. "Get down from there!"

Knowing him to be short on patience and long on memory, they quickly slid down the trench wall and raced to where he stood.

"Forte, I need a runner to go to headquarters," he shouted above the din.

"Wait, captain," interrupted Patsy. "He went the last time. I'll go!"

Domenico thought back. His last trip to *headquarters* was anything but pleasant, and if Patsy wanted to go, why should he argue? He shrugged his indifference.

"Fine, then," said the captain. "Tell them that our artillery is falling short and we need to correct the problem immediately." He paused, scribbled some numbers onto a paper, and then handed it to Patsy. "Here," he continued, "give them these target co-ordinates, and good luck." Paper in hand, Patsy moved out over the back of the slit trench and quickly disappeared beyond its rim. *He's done it to me again,* Domenico suddenly realized. *He'll be a lot safer at headquarters than here in this God-forsaken hole in the ground.*

The shelling stopped precisely at noon, and the ominous silence meant that they would shortly be ordered over the top. Domenico felt the surge of blood pounding in his neck as he grabbed his helmet strap and slid it beneath his chin. With Patsy gone, he would be forced to drag both the machine gun and ammunition boxes to the top of the slit trench alone. He waited for the dreaded command.

Fweep! Fweep! Two staccato blasts from the captain's whistle sent men clamoring into battle along the entire length of the slit trench. The corporal next to him tapped the back of Domenico's helmet and barked, "All right, Forte. This is it!" As Domenico struggled up the trench wall with his weapon and ammunition box, the corporal's lifeless body crashed down upon him, knocking him back to the bottom of the trench.

"Damn you Patsy," he muttered. "The next time I see you, I'm going to flatten your face." He then picked up the corporal's rifle and scrambled up the trench wall.

Initially, the attack went well for the Italians as they moved decisively across the Piave River toward Vittorio Veneto. Domenico's company managed to quickly capture a series of abandoned Austrian trenches—too quickly. By late afternoon, the Austrian-Hungarian forces had recouped and were putting up surprisingly stubborn resistance. As Italian casualties began to mount, Domenico's company, which had served at the point of attack, suddenly found itself cut off from the main body. Shortly before sunset, on the second day of battle, it became clear that they would be unable to hold their position any longer. All around Domenico, men began cursing and slamming their weapons to the ground as they watched the captain walk toward the enemy lines with a large white cloth dangling from the end of his sword.

As Domenico and his comrades were being herded, hands on heads, toward captivity, he glanced down into the ditch that ran along the road that at one time led to headquarters. There, in a contorted lump, lay Patsy's body, riddled by shrapnel. For the rest of his life, Domenico would sob uncontrollably at the mere mention of his friend's name. The war was now over for the both of them, and he would spend the remainder of the conflict in a prisoner-of-war camp.

* * *

Every other day for the last two years, Maria Civita had walked the two kilometers to the post office in Pico and was usually rewarded by a letter from her husband. Suddenly, something had gone terribly wrong; the letters stopped coming. It soon became clear that there would be no more. In desperation, she trekked several miles to a well-known shrine atop Mount Civita. Once there, she knelt silently on the first of a long series of stone steps leading up toward the sanctuary. "Life," she mused, "has been a series of shattered dreams." She had married against her family's wishes and spent the last four years doing penance for it. To make matters worse, two of those years had been without her husband. Now it seemed she might even lose him.

Half blinded by tears, she looked up at the steps, slid off her foot coverings, and began the slow, painful climb on her knees. At each new landing, she lifted her bulky skirt, exposing her knees to abrasive pebbles and grit. At last, upon reaching the top, she rose and reflexively flattened her skirt against her legs and saw that it was covered with blood. She then raised the skirt slightly so as to uncover her knees. The refuse on the steps had torn away the skin from both kneecaps. Blood flowed freely from the open wounds. Numb and void of thought, she then slipped silently into the sanctuary.

Kneeling at the Communion rail before a rack of votive candles, she clung tightly to the few remaining pieces of small jewelry that she had kept from her childhood. As light from the flickering candles danced across an image of the Madonna, a prayer formed on her lips. Slowly, she rose to her feet, inched toward the candle rack, and slipped each piece of jewelry firmly into the offering slot. She then lit a candle, returned home, and waited.

* * *

Despite Domenico's misfortune, the battle of Vittorio Veneto was one of the most decisive of the war. General Diaz's forces would eventually breach the Austro-Hungarian lines in great strength. By capturing Vittorio Veneto, the Italians had dealt a final devastating blow to the Austrian-Hungarian military machine. Germany was now without its most important ally and immediately sued for peace along all other fronts. As a result, in November 1918, an armistice was signed, ending the war in Europe.

After a couple of months in captivity, Domenico once again returned to the farm, where he would remain with Maria Civita for the next four and one-half years. Although it would be their longest time together, nothing had changed. In 1919, a full year after Domenico returned to the farm, they had their second child, a daughter, Concetta. Two years later, they had their third child, a son, Rosario. Although Domenico still had periods of renewed restlessness, they were happy together. By late 1922, however, Domenico and Maria began sensing that events in the larger world might affect their lives. The first sign of trouble surfaced one day as they went into town together to get supplies for the farm. As they walked past some men playing cards, one shouted, "Hey, Domenico, have you seen the newspaper?"

"No. Why?"

"Here. See for yourself." As he attempted to hand the paper to Domenico, it fell to the pavement next to Maria's feet. She picked it up.

"There." He continued, "What do you think now, *Signora*?"

She saw only a disjointed combination of meaningless letters.

She had never been taught how to read. She turned and shoved the newspaper into her husband's hand. "Here! Perhaps you should read it first."

Domenico unfolded the paper.

The large, bold headlines proclaimed, "King Victor Emanuel out. Mussolini in."

"So what does this mean?" asked Domenico.

"It means," snapped the man, "that maybe now we can get veteran's benefits and find work."

"How do you know that?"

"Because this Mussolini says he will make things happen."

Domenico looked at his wife and shrugged. "I already have plenty of work, for what good it's doing me."

While such matters may have been of great importance to the men who played cards, drank wine, and argued at the bistro tables in the village, they were of little consequence to the apolitical Fortes. If a school opened or a new road was built, then the Fascists must be doing a good job. By early 1923, as Domenico watched life on the farm become even more of an economic disaster, he decided to give the United States yet another try. Numbed by the prospect of seemingly endless poverty, Maria Civita quietly surrendered to yet another period of loneliness.

During this next stay in America, some subtle but critical changes occurred that would increase his value in the workplace. He now began to speak passable English and could read well enough to struggle through a newspaper. These skills resulted in better pay, more social flexibility, and broader interaction outside of the Italian-American community. He could now shop, read signs, and, above all, better understand his new culture.

Although he was now consistently able to find work, his visa was about to expire, and he was once more forced to return to the farm. By this time, he had completely rethought his family's life plan. Bolstered by the amount of money that he was able to save in one short year, Domenico resolved that rather than go to America for work alone, on his next trip, he would prepare for his family's emigration and the better life it would mean for them.

Back in the United States, events were unfolding that would

hamper these new plans. During the decade that preceded 1920, over two million Italian immigrants had entered the United States. Now, along with others from Central and Eastern Europe, they were competing with American citizens for a scarcity of jobs and found themselves no longer welcome. In 1921, therefore, President Warren G. Harding signed the Immigration Act into law. It set up a new quota system severely restricting further immigration from these countries.

Entry into the United States was now limited to the privileged, the professionals, and the politically connected. Domenico Forte, the dirt farmer from Pico, was none of these. Because of his track record of acquired job skills, however, he was again able to return to the United States in May of 1925. The purpose of this trip, as stated in the manifest of the *S.S. Conte Verde,* was for him to remain permanently, and for the next four years, he continued to find steady work and sent whatever savings he could accumulate back to Maria Civita.

*   *   *

True to his new life plan, Domenico Forte visited Superior Court in Berkshire County on July 18, 1928, and filed a Declaration of Intent to become a citizen of the United States of America. From 1790 to 1951, an individual intending to become naturalized first filed such a notice (it became voluntary 1952). This meant that after five years, he would be able to petition the court to become naturalized. By late October 1929, his grand vision tumbled down around him as the stock market crashed and the country fell headlong into the Great Depression. Within a year, along with six million other people, he found himself out of work. With his prospects now in shambles, he returned once again to Pico.

Things were no better there. The European economy was soon caught in the ripple effect of the larger economic crisis that infected the rest of the world, and although Mussolini's new policies had, in fact, helped improve the lot of many industrial workers in northern Italy, the poor farm families to the south simply became poorer. Fortunately, Maria Civita had handled money matters prudently and was able to hang onto most of what Domenico had sent to her during the past three years. Still locked into his dream of citizenship, he once again sailed westward across the Atlantic in the summer of 1931. Alone on the farm, with the world in economic and political collapse around her, Maria Civita Forte gave birth to their fourth child, a son, Attilio, in October.

* * *

Work in America was hard to come by, and Domenico would need to show self sufficiency as well as literacy when he eventually petitioned the court. Determined to reestablish his employment record, he crisscrossed the country in search of jobs. He worked for a while as a gandy dancer, repairing railroad tracks throughout the country, and even spent some time in a copper mine in the upper peninsula of Michigan. It was hard, dirty, and dangerous work, but it bought him time and some savings. Finally, on December 27, 1933, Domenico Forte returned to Superior Court in Massachusetts, raised his right hand, and took the oath of citizenship. By this time, Mussolini was dueling with world powers over what he felt were unreasonable disarmament terms forced upon his new ally, Germany, at the end of World War I. The League of Nations promptly rejected his overtures, and his emerging alliance with Nazi Germany was suddenly causing great concern to the rest of the world.

Clearly, Domenico's wandering lifestyle had isolated him from the family. He had not been there for his daughter Concetta's recent wedding, not to mention Angelo or Attlio's entry into the world. His inevitable epiphany would come, however, when he returned to Pico that day in 1935. As he carried his luggage up the narrow dirt roadway leading to the house, he spotted a little boy idly tossing pebbles into a can. After putting his suitcase down, he squatted beside the youngster and asked, "Tell me, little one, what's your name?"

"Forte, signore," he answered, looking up. "Attilio Forte."

"And, how old are you?"

"Four!"

"And what's your papa's name?"

"Domenico."

Stunned, he picked up the child, held him close, and through quivering lips, announced, "I want you to meet your papa!" The collective guilt of all those lost years suddenly crashed through his thoughts. He must act quickly; after all, he was now a citizen and had, once again, found work in America. Domenico made a private vow that they would spend the rest of their lives together.

However well intentioned it may have been, the vow would be short lived. Global events were still unfolding, and the strict immigration laws that were then in place limited those who Domenico could sponsor to immediate family only, meaning only one's spouse and any unmarried children. With his eldest daughter, Concetta, now married and Angelo of military age, the situation was dramatically altered. To make matters worse, Domenico, never a stickler for detail, had neglected to bring the proper certification that he was gainfully employed in the United States. The dream was fast slipping away, and by the summer of 1935, he once more found himself sailing westward alone, in yet another attempt to salvage his affairs. On January 2, 1936, again without her husband by her side, Maria Civita would have their fifth and last child, a daughter, Maria.

While Domenico was still at sea, Benito Mussolini refused to diplomatically reconcile differences and ordered the Italian army which now included Domenico's son, Angelo, to invade Ethiopia. This action triggered a long series of diplomatic crises, and by late October 1936, the United States was firmly embarked on an isolationist path; they wanted no part of war. This resulted in the passage of the Neutrality Act, which essentially forbade the sale of any arms to countries involved in war. This infuriated Mussolini, and brought U.S. and Italian relations to a near breaking point. Mussolini's bad temper, however, was of little concern to Domenico. Ever since he was born, there had been some sort of military crisis in Ethiopia, and this problem would surely go away. His stars still seemed to be reasonably well aligned; after all, the family was in no apparent danger, and he had work. Life, as he saw it, was still salvageable.

Shortly after Domenico's return to the United States, his family also changed dramatically. His daughter, Concetta, no longer at home, provided him with his first grandson, while Angelo would return from the Ethiopian War and marry a young woman from nearby Pontecorvo, Vittoria Raimondi. He was twenty-three and she was twenty-six, and, as was the custom, they took up residence on the Forte farm. During the next couple of years, Concetta had a second son while Vittoria gave birth to their first son, Domenico. This latest addition would be nicknamed Mimino or Little Domenico. The clouds of war were beginning to gather, however, as newspapers in Rome reported that soldiers were once again marshaling in the Eternal City for deployment to the ongoing conflict in North Africa.

All of these changes meant that more living space would be needed, so, using the savings that Domenico had left for their passage, the family set about building a new house. The overall task fell to Rosario and Angelo, along with Domenico's sister, Menica, who proved she could mix mortar and carry cement blocks as well as any man. With the house nearly completed, Rosario carefully chiseled the name "F. D. (Forte Domenico) 1937" into the keystone atop the front door in recognition of its absentee owner.

Meanwhile, global events continued to crimp Domenico's new emigration plan. By late 1939, the Italian government, under Mussolini, had formed a military alliance with Germany, called the Pact of Steel, and in September of that same year, Hitler promptly invaded Poland, setting off World War II. To further complicate matters, Angelo was immediately recalled into the Italian army and once again shipped off to North Africa. Rosario was likewise drafted into the Italian air force and stationed in Bari on the southeastern corner of the Italian peninsula. Domenico's sister, Menica; their elderly parents; Maria Civita; eight-year-old Attilio; three-year-old Maria; Angelo's wife, Vittoria; and their infant son, Mimino, were now all who were left to tend to the farm.

A year later, Concetta had a third son. It would be the last good thing to happen within the Forte family for a long time. In 1940, at Mussolini's order, Italy officially entered World War II and, shortly thereafter, marched into southern Greece. During the four years that an unsuspecting Domenico had spent arranging for the emigration of his family to America, Europe had spun into a black hole. Finally, in May of 1941, the United States suspended diplomatic relations with the Axis powers, and Italy proceeded to overrun the Balkans. Then the Japanese bombed Pearl Harbor. Global events, coupled with Domenico's procrastination, had finally put an end to his dreams, and the Forte family would eventually find itself in grave danger as the scourge of war slowly but surely began grinding its path toward the sleepy, medieval town of Pico.

The Forte family circa 1939. Pictured from left to right. In the back row: Menica (Domenico's sister) and Angelo; in the middle row: Rosario (Domenico's father), Maria D'Anello (Domenico's mother), Vittoria, and Maria Civita; in the front row: Attilio, Domenico (Mimino), and little Maria. Rosario was not present when this picture was taken.

CHAPTER THREE
Memories of a Better Life

*Let us consider the way
in which we spend our lives.*

—Henry David Thoreau

Maria, Sabetta, and Dog had just finished their egg-gathering chores. As they approached the farmhouse, Sabetta paused to admire the building.

"You are lucky to live in such a house," she said.

"Yes," answered Maria. "I was too young to remember them building it, but Mamma talks about it often."

"It's so much nicer than the rickety old shack that my family lives in."

An image of Sabetta's house formed in Maria's mind. Perhaps someday her friend would also have a house like this. As the two girls continued along, Maria surveyed the building with newfound appreciation.

If it were located in a suburb of Naples, the house would hardly be noticed, but situated on the little hill overlooking the sad array of wooden shacks that cluttered the landscape, it was a structure of magnificent proportions. Built of cement blocks and troweled over with a finely pebbled stucco facade, the new Forte home stood three floors high, adorned by a wrought iron balcony rail that provided a dash of elegant contradiction to its otherwise simple lines. Just inside the thick wooden front door, visitors were greeted by a short, narrow hallway. At the end of the hall, an open staircase reached upward to the sleeping area. To the left, there was a generous kitchen, and to the right, the smooth masonry floor of the living area led one's eye to the large, open fireplace that dominated the far wall. It served to both heat the building and to prepare meals. The family had worked hard and spent their money well.

As large and as structurally sound as the house was, there was still no electricity, indoor plumbing, or telephone. There was, however, one new amenity. A small cavity had been built into the back wall, with sliding doors, to accommodate the passage of a chamber pot whose contents would then be deposited far to the rear of the main house. When water was needed for cooking or bathing, it was hauled up from a well at the base of the hill. Evening light came from candles and lamps, and if something more portable was needed outside, a fragment from an old rubber tire, when lit, served nicely. There were no street lights.

Before the big planes came, life on the farm was firmly linked to the earth. Corn, wheat, grapes, and flax were the main crops, but the land also yielded plenty of tomatoes, garlic, onions, lettuce, sweet basil, and parsley—the ingredients that made meals on a mid-century Italian farm so very special.

In addition to the chickens, the rabbits, the dog, and a plow horse, they also raised sheep, pigs, goats, and cows. Besides wool for clothing, the sheep also provided milk to make cheese. After leavening and separating the skim, the milk would be drained and poured into molds to which vinegar, salt, and oil were finally added.

This photo, taken in 1990, shows the Forte home as it was fully restored after the war.

The keystone still remains in the arch over the front door, with the initials that Rosario carved into the stone upon completion of the house.

There was never a shortage of work, and the division of labor evolved from the various skills within the family. Maria's two older brothers, Angelo and Rosario, along with her grandfather, worked the land while her Aunt Menica tended to the larger animals. Maria's mother and grandmother prepared most of the meals while Angelo's wife, Vitorria, who was a seamstress of local renown, made all of the clothing. Maria, meanwhile, saw to the smaller animals, swept floors, and milked an occasional sheep or cow.

The family's intimacy with nature also meant that nothing was wasted or left to chance. When it became necessary to slaughter a pig, the meat was smoked in a little shed away from the house, resulting in a generous yield of sausage, salami, and the ultimate prize, prosciutto. When olives were in season, large drop cloths were carefully positioned around the trees so that, when shaken, the olives fell directly onto them. They were then neatly folded and carted off to the mill for pressing. In the province of Frozinone, a kitchen without olive oil was like a song without words.

In the farmlands of south-central Italy, the barter system also played a major role in the economics of farm life. When the corn was ready for harvest, nearby families would gather at the Forte farm to help shuck the corn and strip it from the cobs. The stripped corn was then brought to a mill for processing so that it could be used for such basic staples as bread and polenta. The rest was dried and used to feed the chickens. Far too much of the family's collective soul had been invested for anything to be wasted. Little Maria fondly remembered the flurry of social activity and camaraderie that accompanied these events, as everyone sang old songs and told older stories well into the evening. The barter was for the labor itself, and when a neighbor's crop was ready, the Fortes would be expected to return the favor, in kind.

Even the grapes were frugally processed. After the children had successfully rescued a portion of the harvest, Angelo, Rosario, and their grandfather would make wine. Once the grapes were crushed and squeezed in a press, the wine would be stored in wooden barrels for fermentation and later poured into large, clear glass jugs. When this had been done, they would then distill the leftover grape skins to make grappa. Whenever the adults drank any of this, they usually became very happy, talked loudly, and sang even louder. Although she was occasionally given a taste of wine at mealtimes, for reasons unbeknown to her, Maria was never allowed to have any grappa. This was not the end of the grape's utility. Her mother would then collect any unused grape skins and line several large pans with alternating layers of grape peels and whole peppers in a stratified concoction that preserved the peppers for months to come.

The earth also yielded more than food. In proportion to the needs of the family, a section of land was set aside each season for growing flax. Once harvested, the women would weigh it down with stones in the nearby stream until it softened and then beat the stalks against rocks in order to remove the crust from the stem. The exposed the fibers were then dried and spun into linen thread for tablecloths and sheets.

Symbolic of their oneness with nature, the people in this farming region had for centuries worn coverings on their feet known as *cioci*. These consisted of pieces of animal skin that, after cleaning and drying, were cut and shaped so as to cover the foot and lower part of the leg. They were then pierced and laced together with long leather strips. By extension of this ancient custom, much of the rural farmland in the province of Frosinone had become known as *La Ciociara*.

As demanding as farm life was, it was also the catalyst that bonded the family together. It generated a common need and sense of purpose which reinforced the love that permeated the Forte farm. All family members knew they were loved and shared that love in return. Work was not so much a chore as it was an act of belonging and contributing to the well-being of the central family. In that sense, it was something that had to be experienced in order to be understood. On some occasions, this intense bonding spilled over beyond family members, as in the case of Maria's dear friend, Sabetta.

Tending to the laundry was more than a chore; it was a social event. Maria would often accompany her mother down to the small stream that flowed near the road at the base of the hill, where neighboring women congregated and chatted as they labored over their laundry. There was one woman in particular who always showed up wearing a bright yellow kerchief on her head and carrying a large load of clothes. *How pretty*, thought Maria. *Perhaps someday, I will have one like that.* The woman was older than her years, and those years had not been kind to her. Widowed young and worn by loneliness, she brought little cheer to the daily stream-side conversation. The other women were aware of her circumstances and took no offense from her predictable depressions. This morning would be no exception.

"*Buon giorno, Signorina.*" The yellow kerchief would nod toward Maria and then quickly shift her attention toward her mother. The war was always at the top of her agenda.

"It has been very quiet in the south—too quiet."

"And is that a bad thing?" answered Maria Civita.

"I hear," she whispered while shooting a glance over her shoulder, "the Germans are moving many large guns and war machines up and down the road from Itri. That means something is going to happen, and it will not be good."

"*Niente male*," cautioned Maria Civita, tapping her fingers across her mouth. "Do you want to frighten the child?"

The yellow kerchief glanced down at Maria. "Yes, I'm sorry. You are right, of course." Silenced for the moment, she turned, lifted her skirt, and waded back to her waiting laundry.

* * *

Maria's fondest memories were also some of the most mischievous. She often thought it great sport to scamper into the cornfield when no one was looking and hide in a crouch, pretending to be lost. The best part of the game was when everyone ran about the rows of corn, calling her name. The only reason that she was ever found was that she giggled uncontrollably all the while she was hiding. One morning, she slipped into Vittoria's room, where the sewing machine was kept, and after fiddling with it for several minutes, managed to stab her finger with the large needle. Half in reaction to her pain and half in fear of being punished, she dashed out into the cornfield and hid—this time for real. It was of little use, however, when she heard her family crying out as they once more navigated through the stalks; she again began giggling uncontrollably. Once discovered, she awaited the punishment that she thought would surely come, only to be handed one very large cookie from a mother whose only concern was that her daughter was safe.

Maria and her six-year-old cousin, Mimino, didn't need gossip from the yellow kerchief to be frightened. Whenever anyone in the family glanced to the south, they could see the naked fear in their faces. No one said much in front of them, and it was this very silence which betrayed them. The first ominous warning came from the *Befana* in January. Local legend had it that an old woman, the *Befana*, went into her village square one day, where she met the three wise men. When she asked them where they were going, they replied, "To find the Christ child."

"Wait for me," she replied. "I want to come with you, but first, I need to get some things from home."

"Very well," they cautioned, "but you must hurry!"

It seems that the *Befana* did not share their sense of urgency and returned to the village, only to discover that the wise men had left without her. The old woman was so distraught that for the rest of her life, she would wander about on the feast of the Epiphany, leaving gifts for all of the children in the hope that she would eventually find the Christ child. The Epiphany came and went this year, without a visit from the *Befana*. There were no nuts, no fruits, no candy—not even a lump of coal for Attilio. *Something was terribly wrong.*

Being Italian also meant being Catholic, and on Sundays or special feast days, the narrow streets near the center of town always took on a decidedly festive atmosphere. The tantalizing aroma of freshly baked pizza beckoned from the shops as men of all ages, protected by umbrellas, played cards for the privilege of determining who would get to drink the wine that waited patiently atop each bistro table. These games were always punctuated by loud protests and animated gestures, which, though dramatic, drew little notice from the nearby pedestrians.

Special church holidays were the most exciting. Maria especially remembered the thirteenth of June because it was the feast of Saint Anthony of Padua, the patron saint of Pico. It was slightly less than a year ago. The ceremony began with a handful of men standing in front of the church, holding a platform bearing a life-size statue of Saint Anthony. As he stood facing the upraised statue, the priest solemnly intoned, *"O glorioso nostra protettore, San Antonio ..."* After completing the prayer for their protector's intercession, he would then dip his aspergillum into a container and snap holy water onto both the statue and the surrounding crowd. On cue, the men then carried the statue through the steep cobblestone streets, led by a gaggle of altar boys. Their pained expressions openly betrayed their collective visceral wish to be somewhere else. What made this occasion so special to Maria was the seemingly endless shower of flower petals that were scattered about the streets along the route of the procession. Standing ankle deep in them, she would wildly toss them into the air as she skipped along behind the crowd.

Through her mind's eye, Maria could also remember the long pilgrimage she once took with her mother and brother Attilio to the Sanctuary of the Madonna della Civita. The shrine was the very one at which Maria Civita had sacrificed her jewelry so many years ago. Although the rumblings of war had not yet reached the mountains to the south, her mother insisted they make the pilgrimage together. Mount Civita was located approximately six miles southeast of Pico, near the town of Itri, and the only way to get there was to walk. Being a day-long trek, this meant that they would have to stay at the shrine overnight and return on the following day. So, with lunches and bedding in tow, off they went down the long, curling Pico-Itri road, toward the shrine.

As they walked, Maria's mother talked about the last war and how their father had served in the Italian army. "It was a bad thing," she recounted. "There was terrible fighting in the north, and I was told that your father was missing in battle. I didn't know if he were dead or alive, so I came to Monte Civita to pray for his safe return, and the Madonna answered my prayers. So, here we are again. Two years ago, your brother Angelo disappeared during the fighting in North Africa, and to this day, we don't know anything about him. I am going to pray, this time, for his safe return, as well as for my little rabbit, Rosario, a radio operator with the air force down in Bari—and so should you." *Her little rabbit*, she mused. He was born with pink skin and pure white hair. His pigmented eyes betrayed his extremely poor vision, but that didn't keep them from dragging him off to war. As an infant, he had reminded her of a rabbit, but as an adult, he had become the strength of the family.

As they continued along the road, a man walking at a rather casual pace emerged from around the bend ahead. Still a distant figure, he paused on their side of the road in order to light his pipe. At that moment, Maria Civita grabbed the children by the hand and pulled them to the opposite side of the road.

"What are you doing?" protested Attilio.

"Never mind," she snapped, "just keep moving and look straight ahead."

"But why?"

"Just do as I say!"

As the man passed by them, he glanced toward the trio, touched the front of his cap, and smiled. Maria Civita's gaze, however, remained locked on the road ahead, and they passed in stony silence. Once he had moved on, she loosened her grip on the children and exhaled a sigh of relief.

"Now," continued Attilio, "can you tell us what that was all about?"

"If you must know," she said, "it's a very serious matter. Many of the men from around here have gone to America to find work, and while they were away, some of their wives found companionship with other men. There are no secrets in a village as small as Pico, and the husbands soon learned of their wives' infidelity. Many husbands abandoned these women and they were forever labeled as *puttani*."

"So, what does that have to do with us?"

"I want no tongues to waggle about me. There will not be even the slightest reason for your father to think in such a way. That means avoiding strange men at all times."

They continued silently along the road for several yards when Maria stopped and tugged at her mother's arm.

"Mamma," she intoned, "when Papa is in America, does he also cross the road?"

Maria Civita took a deep breath then changed the subject.

"Tell me, children," she asked. "What is my name?"

31

'Why it is Mama, of course," answered Maria.

"No, silly," interrupted Attilio. "She means her name is Maria Civita, just like your name is Maria Giuseppa."

"That's right. When I was baptized, I was named after the Madonna that we are going to visit today."

"Why is this shrine so important, Mama?"

"Well, according to the story, a shepherd lost his cow near the top of Monte Civita. It seems also that this particular shepherd was both deaf and dumb. When he finally found the cow, it was kneeling at the base of a large tree. When he looked up, he was surprised to see a picture of the Madonna smiling down at him. Startled, he fell to his knees for a moment and then ran down the mountain and told all of the people about his wonderful vision. Because they all knew that he was afflicted, they were surprised to hear him speak and knew immediately that something wonderful had happened. To commemorate this event, the people built a shrine on the mountain to honor the Madonna. She has since granted many wishes, and we have many wishes to make."

"How long ago did this happen?"asked Attilio.

"Many, many years ago, about the time Columbus sailed to America."

When they finally arrived at the foot of the sanctuary, Maria smiled in relief and turned to face her mother. Suddenly, she felt the sting of a hand across her face. Hurt and confused, she cried, "Mamma, what have I done?"

"Nothing, child, nothing at all."

"I don't understand."

"Don't worry; it will never happen again. It must be done to all who enter this place for the first time."

Maria now questioned the wisdom of making this pilgrimage. Meanwhile, a knowing smirk curled Attilio's lips—after all, it was not his first time.

As they approached the sanctuary, they came upon a long flight of stone stairs, which led up to the chapel itself. Flanked on each side by Maria and Attilio, their mother announced, "These steps are holy, and if we wish to petition the Madonna, we must climb them on our knees." With that, she tugged gently at the children, and they knelt in unison on the bottom step. Attilio, however, had not been blessed with his mother's devotion and was less than thrilled by the prospect of ascending the cold, hard steps on his knees, whatever the spiritual reward. Maria leaned backward and glanced toward her brother, who rolled his eyes, shook his head, and slowly began to rise and move away from the steps. His timing couldn't have been worse. One painful tug on his ear lobe quickly brought him crashing down onto the unforgiving stone step. He would not make this same mistake twice.

With beads laced between her fingers, Maria Civita then blessed herself, and the three pilgrims inched their way up the steps. As they slowly ascended, Maria could hear her mother praying in a distant voice.

"O Maria, madre di Gesu, accogli la mia fervida supplica."

At each new step, she would again stare upward, her face clouded in desperation and repeat, "Oh Maria, mother of Jesus, welcome my fervent prayer." Maria looked up and saw the tears slide down her mother's face. After each recitation, her voice would again become very low, as if to conceal the rest of her petition. Maria strained to hear, but the only word she could make out was *guerra*: war!

They had just returned from the pilgrimage when a random chain of events resulted in the granting of one wish: Rosario was coming home. In July of 1943, the Fascist Party turned against Mussolini, and he was overthrown. Almost immediately, King Victor Emmanuel and Italian Field Marshal Badoglio secretly entered into somewhat shaky negotiations with the Allied command in order to reach an armistice agreement that would, in effect, take the Italian army out of the war. Coincidentally with these negotiations, the Allies were landing in the south, at Salerno. In order to soften the enemy positions there, the attack included extensive air strikes throughout the southern tip of the peninsula, including the airfield where Rosario was stationed. He received back wounds and was immediately furloughed home to recuperate. On the ninth of September, the allies attacked at Salerno and, within hours, the announcement was made that a formal armistice had been signed between the new Italian government and the invading armies. Rosario, who was by then recovering from his wounds back at the farm, no longer had any military unit awaiting his return. Such is the power of prayer.

These are the steps leading to the sanctuary of Maria della Civita. They are the ones that Maria, Attilio, and their mother climbed that spring day in 1943.

Taken circa 1940, this photo shows Angelo Forte (middle, standing with cigarette) with his compatriots in the Italian Army, somewhere in North Africa.

*   *   *

The Church of Sant' Antonio (otherwise known as the *Ciesa Grande* because it was the principle church in town) was the center of religious activity in Pico. Maria would regularly attend Mass there along with her mother and her sister-in-law, Vittoria. The Catholic Mass had for centuries been divided into two major parts: the Mass of the Catechumens and the Mass of the Faithful. The former consists of prayer, scriptural readings, and a homily, while the latter is a replication of events of the last supper, consisting of the Offertory, the Consecration, and the Communion. Once the Mass of the Catechumens is finished, all those who have not yet been baptized would traditionally leave the service in order to receive further catechism instruction. On the other hand, the Mass of the Faithful required obligatory attendance for all practicing Catholics and was usually announced, in the middle of the service, by the ringing of a small set of chimes by an altar boy or an acolyte.

Maria could still see it. No sooner would the chimes ring than the doors at the side of the church would swing open and in would come all of the men who had been playing cards at the bistros in the street. They would reverently remove their caps and kneel, motionless, with bowed heads during the Offertory and Consecration; but once they had received Communion, they would, one by one, quickly retrace their paths from the Communion rail back outside to the waiting card tables. This ecclesiastical shortcut was a regular weekly ritual, and each time, Maria Civita would lean over and whisper into her daughter's ear, "In Pico, praying is women's work." Neither Maria nor her mother could know it, but praying was soon to become everyone's work.

CHAPTER FOUR
Vesuvius Speaks

*And there were flashes of lightning, rumblings,
and peals of thunder, and there was a great
earthquake such as never has been seen since
men were first upon the earth, so great an
earthquake was it.*

—Apocalypse 16:18

It is hard to imagine how a people so sedate, in a setting so pastoral, should suddenly be threatened by the ferocity of war. History tells us that the ancient people of *La Ciociara* have been subjected to conquest many times over many centuries. They all came: the Lombards, the Franks, the Saracens, the Spanish, and finally, the French. If these invaders had anything in common, it was their tendency to do battle on the very ground that now lay beneath the Germans and Allies.

The destruction of the abbey had made the Allied tactical situation worse than before. The rubble produced by the bombing now provided excellent defensive positions for the German paratroops, who were defending the mountain. The Allied ground attacks that followed the bombardment proved equally disastrous, and after several days of some of the most brutal combat in the entire Italian campaign, both sides retired to a stalemate, with no appreciable territorial change.

By mid-March, yet another attack would be ordered, this time in the town of Cassino itself. Nearly five hundred planes of all types were assigned to carpet bomb the town and its immediate surroundings. When it was over, the town no longer existed. As they had done in the abbey atop the mountain, the German defenders once again rushed in to take advantage of the excellent defensive barriers provided by the rubble. By March 25, after disastrous losses on both sides, the line of battle remained essentially unchanged. This new standoff, plus the failed beachhead at Anzio, would force the Allied command to pause and carefully rethink its tactical options.

Given the ghastly carnage that occurred along the Gustav Line it seems entirely appropriate that it also provided the setting for one of the most extraordinary events in the history of World War II. In the late afternoon of March 18, as if in defiant protest against man's insanity, Mount Vesuvius reached deep into the bowels of the earth and erupted in all its fury. Situated approximately sixty miles south of Pico, the twenty-five-thousand-year-old volcano rose menacingly above the same Bay of Naples from which Domenico had sailed so many times. The first eruptions produced a lava flow that cut down everything in its path, including the nearby village of St. Sebastiano. This phase was followed by an eruption of hot ash and cinder, which blackened the skies over the entire central Italian peninsula. Waste also fell upon the villages of Ottavia and San Giorgio, where entire families perished as roofs laden with the ash crashed down upon them. Finally, the eruption changed from a lava flow into a lava fountain, spraying a deadly rain of fire around its base.

The eruption also produced unwelcome military repercussions. Allied field hospitals in the immediate area were forced to evacuate their wounded, regardless of their condition. The severe strain this placed on medical personnel was further compounded by the sudden need to treat the many civilians who were also caught up in the conflagration. Vesuvius was also able to do what the entire German air force had failed to accomplish since the invasion of Italy had begun: destroy an entire American bomber wing. Over eighty planes that had been stationed east of Terzigno were pummeled by hot ash, which destroyed them on the ground.

National Archives and Records Administration
A North American B-25 is silhouetted against the eruption of
Vesuvius on March 23, 1944.

National Archives and Records Administration
A tractor tows a ruined bomber in the wake of the eruption.

In Pico, every person, animal, crop, and house was covered with an abrasive carpet of dust. As the Forte family stood looking up at the darkened sky, they were awed by what appeared to be the glitter of a million fireflies. What they actually saw was the reflection of the sun on the tiny crystallized particles of volcanic ash that hung suspended in the air. Gaping upward, Maria Civita wondered aloud, "Was it a sign? Did the fist of God come crashing to earth in order to crush the obscenity of this war?" It was the grandfather, lost in the past, who remembered witnessing this very scene nearly a half century ago and solemnly announced, "*Sono convinto che sia le vulcano, Monte Vesuvio.*" He knew with certainty that it was, in fact, the volcano, Mount Vesuvius. Finally, on March 28, having flexed its muscles, one of the most dangerous and prolific volcanoes in the world again slipped silently into hibernation.

* * *

The winter campaign along the Gustav Line had seriously drained all the armies involved. In Berlin, military strategists were now focusing on the cross-channel invasion that they knew would be coming soon. As a result, Kesselring watched helplessly as most of the German Luftwaffe in Italy was siphoned off for the defense of Central Europe. This left the Allies in control of the air, and for the next several weeks, Allied bombers continued to pound any roads, bridges, and railways that might be of use to the enemy.

Although Kesselring had brilliantly used the resources at his disposal to delay the Allied advance, it was now clear that the Italian Campaign had become a war of attrition—a war that Germany was losing. Von Senger's crack paratroops were slowly being squandered amid the rubble of Cassino. This, coupled with the loss of division after division to France, made it clear that Italy had become the expendable front. Kesselring's job was to tie up as many enemy resources as possible. By mid-April, Von Senger would advise Kesselring, with some accuracy, that the next Allied assault would likely include the southwestern end of the Gustav Line, as well as Cassino.

Von Senger was also responsible for the defense of the entire southwest sector of the Gustav Line. His corps, which included the paratroops at the monastery, was now stretched over an eighty-mile front. His responsibilities also included the creation of a second line of defense ten miles to the rear. Operating out of a castle headquarters in nearby Roccasecca, he organized and fortified what would become known as the Hitler Line. An unsuspecting Pico was to become its critical pivot point.

All previous attempts to penetrate the Gustav Line had failed, in part because they had been conducted at narrow, local points along the line and had thus enabled Kesselring to move elements of his armies around at will. He was primarily able to do this via the Pico-Itri road, the very road along which Maria Civita had taken her children on pilgrimage to the shrine less than a year ago. A plan was then proposed by French General Alphonse Juin that would strip Kesselring of this advantage by broadening the attack. The Allied command agreed and immediately set about organizing a new assault scheme based upon Juin's suggestion. The attack was set for May 11, 1944.

* * *

After a winter and spring of continuous fighting, nearly everyone in Pico knew that the sword of Damocles now hung menacingly over their heads. The roads to and from the tiny *paese* were constantly clogged with German military traffic, but even if these roads were accessible to civilians, the people were reluctant to leave. Pico was everything. For centuries, it had been the stabilizing center of their culture and their faith. At the most basic level, it was the essence of their existence: their homes, their shops, their farms, and their livelihoods. To a few, the battle line at Cassino appeared to be stalled, meaning that perhaps they would remain safe. This assumption was made all the more reasonable by the fact that the Germans had not yet issued a civilian evacuation order, and they most certainly would do so if danger were imminent. Besides, Pico was in the middle of nowhere and appeared to be absolutely useless from a military standpoint.

The major contradiction to this psychological opiate was the steadily increasing presence of the German army in and around the little town. For the majority of Picanos, this harsh reality dashed the myth that they would remain safe much longer. Kesselring's plan to establish a secondary line of defense had already been put into motion. The Germans knew they must maintain control of the Pico-Itri road, and since Pico also contained the critical crossroads to Ceprano and Pontecorvo, it was the linchpin to the entire plan and must be held at all cost. If Pico was the heart of the German defensive strategy, the Pico-Itri road was its aorta.

CHAPTER FIVE
The Colonel and the Chickens

*Among beings there are some more and
some less good, true, noble and the like.*

—St. Thomas Aquinas

Maria and Sabetta watched as the adults washed and rinsed several large glass jugs, which were normally used to store wine. After they had dried in the sun, Maria was assigned to hold a paper funnel in place as corn meal and flour were carefully poured into the jugs, which were then tightly corked. This process was then repeated, without the funnel, using cheese and sausage. Maria also helped her mother fill canning jars with tomatoes and stack them into heavy wooden crates.

Once the foodstuffs were prepared, Rosario then set about the task of burying the whole lot. Systematically, he moved about the farm, selecting spots that would attract the least attention. After each internment, he would mark the location on a piece of paper and cover the spot with a layer of sod in order to conceal the freshly dug earth. For good measure, he then marked each spot with a coded arrangement of stones that he would share with the rest of the family. It took three precious days.

*   *   *

In the motorcycle sidecar at the head of the column, the German officer leaned over, touched his driver's shoulder, and motioned him to pull over. The sergeant nodded dutifully, signaled to the truck behind him, and swung to the side of the road. As if choreographed, the entire convoy turned in unison behind him. Quickly, the driver jumped from the motorcycle and raced around to open the sidecar door. Neither man noticed the two young girls who had been fetching water from a nearby well, nor did they see them drop their buckets and scamper behind a tree. Maria and Sabetta crouched motionless and listened as the two men spoke. After a brief exchange, the driver then turned and ran down the road toward the long line of trucks.

Slowly, Maria and Sabetta raised their heads, their eyes fixed on the man who seemed to be in charge as he stepped slowly away from the sidecar and looked down at the long column of vehicles that, at his bidding, now sat motionless beside the road.

"Maria," gasped Sabetta, "who are these men?"

"I don't know. They are some kind of soldiers."

"I think you're right, but I can't understand them."

After a couple of minutes, two other men joined the sergeant, and the three of them walked briskly forward along the line of trucks. The girls watched as the one in charge reached into the back seat of the sidecar, pulled out a large paper, unfolded it, and spread it across the fender of the lead trunk. After pinning it to the fender with his cap and gloves, he moved his finger rapidly over the paper. Suddenly, pausing for effect, he defiantly jabbed his finger into the map and shouted the only word the children could understand: "Pico!" He then turned and squinted past where the girls were hiding, pointed up the hill toward the farmhouse, and began refolding the large paper. As the small assembly disbanded, the girls saw that no one was paying any attention to them and raced back to the barn, where they found Rosario feeding the plow horse. He was in the military; he would surely be able to explain all of this.

"Rosario," they cried, "men are coming up the road. Who are they?"

Maria's brother moved to the barn door and squinted out into the morning sun.

"*Tedeschi*," he moaned. "*Tedeschi soldati*."

"That's what German soldiers look like?"

"Yes! I knew many of them in Bari."

No sooner had he spoke than the motorcycle carrying the two men skidded to a halt in front of the farm house. Alerted by the clamor, Maria Civita and Vittoria rushed outside just as the sergeant bounced from the bike.

"*Buon giorno, Signora*," he intoned, looking directly toward Maria Civita.

"*Buon giorno, Signore*," she responded. "You speak Italian."

"Yes!" he replied, as he opened the door to the sidecar, enabling the other man to step out. Apparently a soldier of considerable authority, he emerged deliberately, his cold eyes glaring out from behind an otherwise mechanical expression. Immediately, he began slapping his gloves into the palm of one hand as if marking cadence for his mechanical pace. He was obviously interested in the house itself. Seemingly satisfied, he moved back toward where the family had gathered and glanced at them with the indifference of one inspecting a cord of wood. As he reached Rosario, he jerked erect, his eyes locked on the young, white-haired figure standing before him. His indifference suddenly turned into rage. He snarled something at the driver, who moved obediently to where Rosario stood.

"My colonel wishes to know," he snapped, "what a German soldier is doing in this hovel. Where is your uniform and why aren't you with your unit?"

"German? I'm not German. This is my home and this is my family. I was born here."

"He won't believe you. He says you must be a deserter and can't decide whether to return you to your command or have you shot immediately."

"I'm not German, I tell you. I am an Italian, an *albino Italiano*. I was stationed in the air force and wounded in the back during the raids near Bari."

The sergeant reached out and yanked Rosario's shirt upward. Upon seeing the scars, the colonel waved his hand in dismissal and snapped once more at his driver.

"Very well," said the sergeant. "You people can't make up your minds which side you're on, anyway; therefore, your loyalties are of little consequence to us. By the way, the colonel also wishes to inform you that this is where he will be staying."

"And if we say no?" interrupted Maria Civita.

"*Signora*, no one says no to a colonel, unless, of course, you are a general."

Indifferent to the conversation, the colonel brushed away the heavy accumulation of dust from his coat, spoke to the sergeant at some length, and stepped back into the sidecar. The sergeant then returned to face Maria Civita. "It has been a long drive from Itri," he continued, "and we have been showered by the filth from your miserable volcano. The colonel wishes for me to inform you that we shall also require laundry services while we are here."

"Since you asked so nicely," conceded Maria Civita, "of course we will." She wondered if the colonel had a heartbeat.

Standing at the edge of the gathering, little Maria tugged at her brother's sleeve and whispered, "Rosario, isn't Itri near Monte Civita?"

"Yes. So what?"

"Do you suppose the colonel has ever visited the shrine to the Madonna?"

"How should I know?"

"Well, if he did, I'll bet no one slapped his face."

The sergeant managed to suppress the smile that began forming on his lips and chose not to translate the child's observation; instead, he turned and merely related the success of his negotiations to the colonel, who grunted something under his breath and then waved an arm toward the road. As he remounted the motorcycle, the sergeant turned toward the family and added, "Oh yes! There is one final thing. We will be placing some anti-aircraft guns at the base of the hill. That means there will be soldiers stationed there. For your own safety, you are not to go near them."

"How then do you expect us to do your precious laundry?" Maria Civita protested. "The guns will be right next to the stream!" The sergeant relayed her grievance to the colonel, who nodded his assent.

"All right, *Signora*," the sergeant continued, "but when you go there, do your business quickly and then leave."

"We understand."

"Very well. As for now, we have duties to attend elsewhere, but we'll be back by nightfall."

Having successfully rearranged priorities on the Forte farm to their liking, the two men raced back down the dusty farm road toward the town of Pico.

*   *   *

The colonel had only been settled in for a week when Maria and Sabetta discovered the theft. It was mid-morning, and they had just finished gathering eggs when Sabetta noticed that her apron seemed lighter than usual.

"Look, Maria," she said. "There's not as many today."

"Do you suppose, we missed some hens?"

"No. We got them all, even the ones in the haystack."

"Let's count the eggs then."

"Good idea."

One by one, they gently lifted the eggs from Sabetta's apron and placed them on the ground.

"*Undici, dodici, tredici.* Thirteen! There are only thirteen eggs!"

The girls hurried into the kitchen to share their startling discovery.

"Yes, Mama," Maria confirmed, "we counted them, twice, and then we counted the chickens."

Maria Civita wiped her hands on her apron and then stiffened. She knew. "Come, girls, we are going down to the stream to wash *Monte Vesuvio* from the colonel's uniform."

Armed with the dirty clothes and some soap, they walked down to the stream just below the artillery emplacement. The woman with the bright yellow kerchief was already there, rinsing some things out. She spoke first.

"I see," she noted, looking at the soiled officers uniform, "that you are working for the *Tedeschi* today."

"We do what we have to do," answered Maria Civita as her gaze wandered toward the gun emplacement where the soldiers were now filling bags with sand and building walls with them. "You stay here and wet these things down," she told the girls. "I'll be right back." Carefully, she folded the colonel's clothes so that the epaulets clearly showed and marched toward where they were working.

"Halt!" said one. "Weren't you told to stay away from this place?"

"*Si,*" she continued, extending the jacket toward him, "but we live in that farmhouse up on the hill, and we were told that it would be all right for us to wash this officer's clothes in the stream."

Once he saw whose uniform it was, his tone suddenly mellowed.

"Of course, *Signora*," he said. "Wash whenever you like," but for your own safety, please don't come this close to the guns again." It was when he turned away that Maria Civita spotted the charred remains of a camp fire and the chicken bones scattered around it.

"*Grazie*," she replied and returned to where Maria and Sabetta waited by the stream.

"Well," asked the woman in the bright yellow kerchief, "what was that all about?"

"*Tedeschi*," she said. "They like to eat other people's chickens."

*   *   *

Once the colonel inspected the town, he was pleased at Von Senger's choice for a second line of defense. Built on the side of a hill, the town itself was tightly compacted, and its steep, narrow streets offered few, if any, places for large-scale troop movement. In addition, the ancient town also had a valuable medieval fortification. The old castle, with its walls and towers still intact, sat atop the end of the Via del Castello at the northernmost edge of town. For good measure, the ground outside of town would lend itself very nicely to the portable pill boxes he would be installing. This defensive advantage was further complemented by the cemetery, which stood on high ground just outside of town. It contained a church, which rose above everything and would provide excellent visual command of the entire area. Noting the hour, he ordered the sergeant to drive him back to the farm.

When they arrived at the house, but before he could get out of the sidecar, the colonel looked up and saw Maria Civita standing in the doorway with folded arms and anger etched into her face.

"Sergeant," he snapped, "find out what's wrong with that woman."

The sergeant quickly became engaged in a long, animated

conversation, which ended with his dejected return to the sidecar. "Well, sir," he said, "it seems that she washed clothes today."

"And why is that any of my concern?"

"They were your clothes, sir, but there *is* more to it."

"Go on!"

"It's about their chickens, sir."

"Chickens?"

"Yes, sir, chickens. Is seems that ever since our men have been in the area, their chickens have been mysteriously disappearing, and they wondered if you could ..."

*   *   *

Maria Civita was alarmed by the colonel's outburst as he suddenly began shouting and gesturing toward the doorway where she stood. She instantly regretted the foolishness of confronting someone who had such power and authority. She stumbled backward into the house, but they had already spun the motorcycle around and were bouncing at breakneck speed, back down the hill. *Tuitt i santi prega per me! What have I done?* There had been some talk about civilians being killed for far less than she had just done. If they shot her, what would happen to her family? It would not be long before she found out. Within minutes, the sergeant returned alone, dismounted, reached into the sidecar, and pulled out a long, narrow sign lettered in German. Borrowing a ladder from the barn, he mounted the sign over the front doorway. His work finished, he stepped back and announced, "There! That should do it."

"What does it say?" asked the puzzled woman.

"'Commandant Panzer Grenadier Regiment.' Every soldier for miles around now knows that these premises are under the colonel's personal protection."

Numbed with relief, she gestured toward the sign and said, "So, sergeant, your colonel really does have a soft spot somewhere inside of him."

"Soft spot? I hardly think so."

"How else do you explain his helping us like this?"

"Helping *you*? Not at all! You forget, *Signora*, that when the men

49

steal your chickens, they are also stealing his breakfast eggs. Now, I must go back into town and fetch him. When I left, the colonel was screaming at a rather petrified artillery captain." He smiled slightly, as though amused by the thought, then turned and mounted his motorcycle.

Indeed, for as long as the colonel remained, no chicken would ever again be taken prisoner by the German army.

CHAPTER SIX
The Bombs Fell: May 11–14

I've been through two wars and I know.
I've seen cities and homes in ashes.
I've seen thousands of men lying on the
ground, their dead eyes looking up at the skies.
I tell you, war is hell.

—Gen. William Tecumseh Sherman

From one of his corps headquarters near the bombed-out rubble that was once the birthplace of St. Thomas Aquinas, Von Senger prepared for the assault that he knew would surely come. His generalship and stubborn resistance along the Gustav Line had also made him a military celebrity, and in April, he was ordered to return to Germany so that he might be decorated by Hitler himself. Before leaving, Von Senger cautioned Kesselring that he felt the rugged terrain would preclude any major assault through the Aurunci Mountains, but the next attack might well involve the southern coastal flank. Kesselring agreed, and in early May, with Von Senger no longer at the front, the stage was now set for the fourth and final battle of Cassino to begin. At precisely one hour before midnight on May 11, 1944, in an attack timed to catch the German defenders outside of their bunkers, Allied artillery let loose along the entire Gustav Line. The shelling continued well into the next day, at which time it was augmented by simultaneous Allied air raids.

*   *   *

Jarred awake by the sudden roar from the not-so-distant artillery, families throughout the Liri Valley rushed outside. Gun flashes and explosions lit the night air across the entire horizon. This wasn't like the previous attacks or the eruption of Vesuvius. It was much worse. Maria bolted upright from where she lay sleeping between her mother and aunt. The staccato flashes of light through the window lit the bedroom well enough for her to clamber across the room and peer outside. "Mamma, Zizi," she cried, "Come here and see for yourself!" The women rose and stumbled across to the window, where they were unceremoniously jerked awake by what seemed like a midnight sun. They quickly dressed and rushed downstairs. As they moved past the room where the colonel and sergeant had been sleeping, Maria paused to look inside. A small kerosene lamp glowed on the table, and the colonel sat on the edge of his bed, pulling on his boots. The sergeant, meanwhile, was crouched in a corner, feverishly cranking the handle on a small square box.

Once outside, the family gaped in awe at the southern sky. The mountain peaks were silhouetted against the flashing glow of landing shells and phosphorous flares, which lit up the night along the entire horizon. Maria Civita was the first to speak. "What is happening?"

"This time," answered Rosario, "they mean business."

From inside the house, they heard the colonel shout something to the sergeant; then they stepped aside as the two men rushed out the front door towards the motorcycle. Seconds later, they were racing, at full tilt, down the hill towards Pico.

* * *

Rosario was right. At that very moment, the Allies had unleashed twenty-one divisions against the German positions. At the center of this line stood General Alphonse Juin's French Expeditionary Corps, ready to advance along a line that included the Aurunci Mountains. The Allies had correctly assumed the mountain range would be the most lightly defended sector of the German lines; nevertheless, it in no way reduced the enormity of the job given to the FEC.

Juin's corps consisted of roughly one hundred thousand Free French and Algerians, along with approximately twelve thousand Moroccan Goumiers. For much of the early twentieth century, the French, who already controlled Algeria, became mired in a series of conflicts for control of Morocco. Many of these clashes occurred in the rugged Atlas Mountains of southern Morocco. After nearly twenty-two years of Moroccan pacification, the ruthless battlefield tactics of the Goumiers had earned them a reputation—however notorious—as the most dangerous mountain fighters of their day. It was hardly surprising, therefore, that when the Allies eventually recaptured Morocco in 1942, that these men would become a critical element of Morocco's contribution to the French Expeditionary Corps.

Some of these Goumiers quickly gained attention within the Allied ranks for their sometimes brutal treatment of both captives and civilians. Prisoners were said to be sodomized and murdered, while rape and plunder were often the fate those civilians who were unfortunate enough to be caught in their path. To say that they were irregulars would be an understatement. Dressed in long, striped, robelike uniforms and WWI-styled helmets, each Goumier was armed with a rifle and a long, sharp knife, which he was more than adept at using. It was these hardened men, led by superbly trained French officers (who hated the Germans) who waited, along with their pack animals, for the advance to begin.

On the morning of May 12, the Goumiers, who until this point had been held in reserve, were released across the Garigliano River. By evening, they had reached Castleforte, which the French had already taken along with Monte Maio and Appollinare. Except for these modest gains, however, most of the pieces had yet to fall into place.

On the next day, the Moroccan Goumiers captured Spigno. This would prove to be a decisive breach of the Gustav Line in that it enabled them to gain access to the passes leading to the Aurunci Mountains. When the people of Spigno came out of hiding to greet the advancing Goumiers, the women were raped and their homes were looted. By the end of the day, with Spigno now in their wake, the rather strange-looking caravan of twelve thousand men and four thousand mules continued to wind its way through the valley leading north into the most formidable natural barrier the Allies would face: the Aurunci Mountains.

* * *

As they had done every day for the last several weeks, the German soldiers near the stream were once again busy cleaning volcanic ash from their anti-aircraft pieces. This tiresome "make work" ritual was usually accompanied by a good deal of cursing and mumbling, but today, they labored in silence. The noise of battle to the south had riveted their attention to the task at hand; the condition of their weapons could now mean life or death. At the top of the hill, Rosario had just completed a tour of the food burial sites along with his mother, explaining to her each of the stone arrangements and pointing them out on his map. As they stood in front of the house, listening to the cannonade that roared behind the mountains, their gaze gradually shifted down toward the German gun emplacement.

"Too close, Ma," he complained. "They are much too close."

"I know," she nodded, "but there is nothing we can do about it except move ourselves."

At that moment, the noonday sun broke through. "Rosario," she squinted skyward, "something good is happening."

"At any other time, I might agree with you," he cautioned as he pointed to a tiny speck in the sky, "but look up there." Quickly, the spot became a small plane. It had neither bombs nor guns. Down at the bottom of the hill, the Germans threw down their cleaning rags and quickly began pulling camouflage netting over the guns. The little plane now droned overhead in ever-shrinking circles, moving lower with each turn.

"What's it doing?" she asked.

"It's an observation plane, and if he spots anything down here that looks suspicious, there's going to be hell to pay."

"The soldiers have rifles. Why don't they just shoot him down?"

"They can't. If they try, they will give away their position, but that's none of our concern. Hurry, let's get everyone into the house."

As they rushed to warn the family, Maria Civita glanced upward. The little plane was now directly above the German gun positions. As it curled slowly downward, a flash of sunlight reflected from the artillery barrels. She froze. The Germans had cleaned their guns to a fault. Did the people in the little plane see that? As if to allay her fears, the plane turned into a sweeping arc and droned away. Perhaps they would be safe after all.

The bombers came at precisely two o'clock. On the first pass, the bombs crashed into the fields along the roadway, causing the earth to convulse around the farmhouse where the family huddled together. Pieces of shrapnel ricocheted across the stucco façade, spitting chunks of plaster into the yard. At the base of the hill, a direct hit tossed two of the big guns out into the roadway as if they were plastic toys. The bombardment continued for several minutes, filling the air over the farm with smoke. Then, as quickly as it had begun, the raid was over. Emboldened by the silence, the family inched their way outside of the house, where they watched as the soldiers slowly came out of hiding. Down in the river bed, a bright yellow kerchief, soaked with blood, bounced gently among the rocks as it floated downstream. World War II had arrived in Pico.

As brief as it was, the bombing raid had dramatically altered the landscape. Large craters now pocked the fields where crops once stood. Not far from the house, the plow horse lay motionless on his side, his legs sticking outward much like a table that had been kicked over and abandoned. Smoldering bomb fragments filled the air with the acrid stench of burnt metal. So extensive was the destruction that it was impossible to tell where the bombing started and where it ended.

Maria Civita stood for several minutes, studying the ruin, and then suddenly remembered her daughter, Concetta. *Dear God, is she dead or alive? What about her husband and children?*

"I need to go to your sister's home. Now," she announced to Rosario.

"Ma, that's crazy. Look around you. You'll be dead before you reach the roadway."

"You don't understand. I must find out if they are safe."

"And what if the planes return? You don't really believe they've left for good, do you?"

"It doesn't matter. Your sister is in danger. I must know if she is all right," she cried, as she turned and raced down the hill.

In order to reach her daughter's home, she would have to pass near the bombed-out German gun position. As she approached, she could see that a large part of the emplacement had been destroyed. What was left of two large artillery pieces had been blasted out into the roadway, much to the frustration of the long German truck convoy that had just come up the Pico-Itri road with reinforcements. Men milled excitedly about, pulling the dead and wounded from the wreckage while a Tiger tank rattled into position and began bulldozing the snarled mess from the roadway.

Indifferent to their plight, she continued on to her daughter's home, where she found everyone safe. Armed with this knowledge, she immediately set about to return home. It was when she again passed by what was left of the German gun positions that it happened. The soldiers were already pointing skyward. It was back! The little plane was back and already descending in tight circling patterns. When it was no more than few hundred yards over their heads, she watched as it leveled off just above the long German column stalled in the road. The sudden volley of rifle fire startled her. The Germans knew that they had been spotted, and there was no point in playing possum this time around. Their effort was in vain, however, as the plane quickly descended behind the shoulder of a nearby foothill.

I should have listened to Rosario. She had only gone but a few hundred yards when she caught sight of two young men running toward a nearby barn. They were the Rossi brothers, Enrico and Alberto. The two often hired out as day laborers on the farms around Pico. When they were within a few yards of the building, they spotted her and stopped. While Enrico gasped for air, Alberto, the younger of the two, yelled out through cupped hands, "Signora Forte, come with us. We will all be much safer inside."

"No," she shouted. "I must get home."

"You'll never make it," he said as he waved his arm in a beckoning sweep. "The planes will be here soon."

"No. Thank you, but no!"

Alberto shrugged toward his brother, and the two men disappeared into the barn.

No sooner had they parted than a new formation of planes rose from beneath the southern horizon. *How did they get here so quickly?*

Knowing for certain that death would once again be raining

down, she quickened her pace across the large field. It was too late. The first explosion caused the ground to resonate beneath her feet. Clutching the hem of her skirt, she now ran wildly through the tall grass. The bombs continued to chew large, gaping holes into the field ahead of her. Flying dirt stung at her skin, forcing her to the ground. In the roadway below, soldiers scrambled from their trucks, dove into ditches, and watched helplessly as the suddenly vulnerable tank tried to pull away from the wreckage.

Half crazed by the thought of what might be happening to her family and half numbed by the knowledge that she would surely die in this place, Maria Civita was brought to her feet by a terror-induced surge of adrenaline. As she stumbled ahead, a second wave of planes filled the sky. Startled and directionless, she froze. Suddenly, the concussion from a nearby explosion tossed her, in a disjointed pirouette, through the air and onto the edge of a massive bomb crater. Stunned, she was unable to rise beyond her knees and elbows. Her ears rang, and a pain burned in her hip. Out of the corner of her eye, she spotted her kerchief. It had fallen off and now lay at the bottom of the hole.

Void of coherent thought, the most important thing she could do with the rest of her short life was to die wearing that kerchief. From her semi-kneeling position, she leaned sideways and tumbled with abandon to the bottom of the hole, deafened by the thunderous explosions around her. Shrapnel and debris spit across the top of the hole and ricocheted against the upper edges, sending little geysers of soil into the air. *It might have been better if the colonel had shot me.* With every molecule in her trembling body, she pressed her face against the bottom of the crater and clutched at the loose dirt, which, indifferent to her plight, merely squeezed out from between her fingers.

Suddenly, there was silence. The planes were gone.

Gagging on dirt, she crawled up the wall of the hole and managed to struggle upright in order to see what was left of the world. Back at the road, the smoldering wreckage of the tank had become part of the grotesque pile of debris. The now burning convoy lay in varying stages of ruin for as far as she could see. After wiping grime from her eyes with the tattered kerchief, she looked back toward the barn where the Rossi brothers had taken refuge. It was gone. In its place, there were a few smoldering planks and what appeared to be pieces of bodies. No longer able to run, she snapped dirt from the kerchief, knotted it around her head with trembling fingers, and then stumbled numbly off in the general direction of the farm.

*   *   *

The military records of the U.S. 12th Air Force for May 13, 1944, stated, in part, "B-25s blasted towns in rear of battle lines, with good results, at Pastena, Pico, Vallecorso, and Itri."

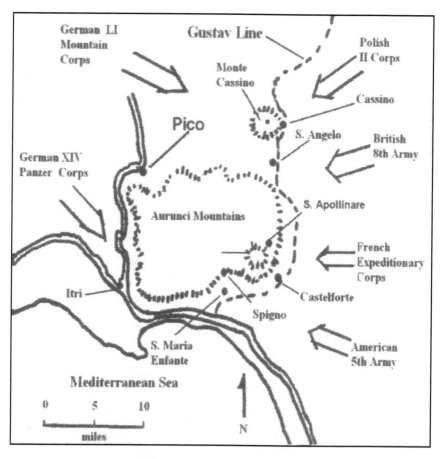

The early stages of the attack
on the Gustav Line, May 11–14, 1944.

CHAPTER SEVEN
False Hope on the Home Front

All I know is what I read in the newspapers.

—Will Rogers

"Night desk. Foley here!"

"Chuck, this is Fred Philips. How's my big shot reporter friend?"

"Fred? Hi, buddy. I'll bet it's been more than six months. When are you and Joan going to come visit us so we can show you around the big city?"

"Not anytime soon. It's nearly a three hour drive, and we'll never make it with our measly gas ration coupons."

"Yeah, tell me about it. So, to what do I owe the honor of this call?"

"Listen, Chuck, I'm in charge of the second-shift assembly operation here at the plant, and my crane hitcher, Domenico Forte, who happens to be sitting directly across the desk from me, has a serious problem. It seems he has a family in Italy, and he's very upset by the war reports. Like the rest of us, he's living on day-old news, so I told him that I had a friend in the newspaper business who might be able to help him."

"Go ahead. It's your nickel."

"The headlines we're seeing deal with a massive offensive going on in Italy along this thing called the Gustav Line, which Domenico tells me is only a few miles from where his family lives."

"And where might that be?"

"A place called Pico."

"Never heard of it, but let me look through this atlas I keep at the ready. Let's see ... Pico ... Pico. Where in hell is Pico? Ah, there we are. I've got to tell you, Fred, this dot on my map is so small that there are probably more people in this news room than live there."

"So, what can you tell me?"

"Like your man said, it appears to be about fifteen kilometers behind the Gustav Line, in the foothills of a huge mountain range. From what's being reported, it doesn't appear to be in any direct line of attack, but that was yesterday's news."

"What's the latest you've got?"

"Let me look. I've got a pile of stuff from the wire services right here on my desk that I haven't touched yet. Well, will you look at that?"

"Look at what?"

"Bucky Walters, you know, the right hander for Cincinnati, was pitching a perfect game against the Braves when this Boston hitter, Connie Ryan, ruins everything with a broken bat single. Can you imagine that? A broken bat sin—"

"Chuck?

"What?"

"The war, Chuck?"

"Yeah. Sorry. The stuff that you'll read in tomorrow's paper won't tell much more than you already know about movement at the front. The British and Indians have managed to gain a foothold across the Rapido River at the town of Cassino, but the Poles are catching hell storming the monastery—or rather, what's left of it. Down along the coast, the Americans are slugging it out in a couple of towns named San Pietro and Santa Maria Infanti. It seems that the real estate keeps changing hands, and there is nothing left to Santa Maria Infanti but a pile of rubble."

"Yeah, but what about Pico?"

"It's more along the line where the French are moving. They are reporting some progress and appear to have captured a place named Ausonia. Let's see ... Ausonia is down here, and Pico is up there. Well, that's good news."

"What is?"

"This Pico place is in the northern foothills of one of the most treacherous mountain ranges in all of Italy. In order to attack at that point of the line, the French would have to cross the entire length of that range."

"That's a problem?"

"A huge problem. Let me tell you Fred, back in the thirties, when I was in Rome covering the Mussolini-Hitler thing, I passed through that area several times, and I can assure you, it would be impossible for a mountain goat to navigate through there, let alone an attacking army. Furthermore, these Aurunci Mountains stand directly between the French army and this Pico place. It would seem to me that the real prize at the moment is Rome itself, and that's where they will concentrate the attack. What possible reason would they have to get tied up in a side show in that little hole in the wall?"

"Are you certain?"

"The mountains make it certain; besides, I can read a map."

"Okay, I'll share this with Domenico."

"Good luck, buddy, and don't forget, that invitation is always open."

Fred Philips placed the phone back into its cradle, spun his chair around, and smiled at his nervous crane hitcher. "Relax, Domenico. I think you're going to like what he said."

* * *

Six time zones away, the Goumier mountain fighters, stripped of everything except their rations, rifles, and knives, began leading their pack animals up the four-thousand-foot Monte Stampadora. Their target: the Pico-Itri road. They were in their element at last!

National Archives and Records Administration
Dressed in a striped djellabal, a Moroccan Goumier sharpens his
koumia, or knife, prior to the campaign on mainland Italy.

CHAPTER EIGHT
The Day the General Came

Nothing can be more important than
that the work of a soldier be well done.

—Plato, *The Republic* [2]

While it is certainly true that Field Marshal Albert Kesselring could read a map far better than Chuck Foley, he nevertheless came to the same conclusion—namely, that the Aurunci Mountains were impenetrable. Accordingly, he made only a modest troop commitment to the area, and, so far, events were proving him to be right. The German army was being hit hardest on its two flanks. This meant that the secondary Hitler Line, anchored at Pico, might prove no more than a necessary precaution. Still, two things nagged at him as he paced about his headquarters in Monte Soratto. First, there were conflicting reports from the front; who was he fighting and where were they? Second, where was Von Senger? He should have been back from Berlin by now. He snatched at the ringing field phone.

"Kesselring."

"Von Senger here!"

"Frido? Where are you?"

"Not far from Cassino, and things look bad. We're being hit by the British at Cassino and by the Americans along the coast."

"So? We expected that."

"It's the French that bother me."

"What about them?" Kesselring's tone was becoming impatient.

"I have no idea where they are. I have only sketchy reports about some encounters around San Giorgio, but nothing concrete."

---

2   Jowet B, trans. *Plato's Republic*. New York: Random House, p. 67.

"San Giorgio ... that's along the southern edge of the mountains. That has to be a diversion."

"That could be, but if I am to establish any kind of holding action, I will need reinforcements immediately."

"What did you have in mind, Frido?"

"One panzer division would be a good start."

"And where would I get one?"

"From Anzio."

"Absolutely not! If I weaken the line at Anzio, the enemy will surely break out."

"But, general ..."

"But nothing, Frido. Is there anything else?"

"Well, sir," Von Senger hesitated, "then I request permission to pull back."

"No! Berlin expects us to hold the Gustav Line at all costs. If that's clear, then you have your orders." Kesselring slowly positioned his phone over its cradle and let it drop into place.

*   *   *

By the seventeenth, Von Senger had seen enough. He had lost nearly two divisions, and his men in Cassino and at the abbey were about to become cut off. His worst nightmare had come true, and Kesselring still forbid his withdrawal from those positions. His frustration was further fuelled by reports that Moroccan Goumiers were now clamoring down Monti Fogetta and stood poised to capture the Pico-Itri road. Everything now hinged on making a stand at Pico.

As he raced toward Pico in his shrapnel-riddled Volkswagen, he was greeted by bombed-out roads and bridges. The closer he got to Pico, the worse the destruction. About a mile out of town, he stopped and got out in order to survey the damage. The countryside was in ruin. The raids had nearly crippled his planned troop movements. He walked briskly back toward the driver, who was still holding the door open, tapped his shoulder with his baton, and said, "Get me into Pico at once!"

*   *   *

Back at the farm, Little Maria and her family huddled against a wall in an upstairs room. She covered her ears against the deafening thunder of the bombs as they methodically chewed up what was left of the countryside. Almost as though it were immune from destruction, the farmhouse was the only structure still standing within a half-mile radius. It was also all that separated the family from certain death, but because of its closeness to the German positions, it was unlikely that it could save them much longer. The bombs were coming ever closer to the house. Blasts of dirt and shrapnel chewed away at the walls, spitting shards of glass into the room, past where Maria crouched. At that very moment, a bomb crashed to earth less than thirty feet from the front door—and by some miracle, failed to detonate.

*   *   *

Dusk finally marked the end of the bombing, and the sergeant now sat on the front stoop, smoking a cigarette. From his vantage point, he could also see the colonel personally supervising the removal of the wreckage from the roadway. Gradually, his gaze wandered about the front yard. There would be no more problems about chickens because there was simply no more henhouse. A few yards away, the hot Italian sun was making slow work of the unfortunate plow horse as it lay near the edge of a large bomb crater. As for the crops, there was nothing left. Only short, burnt stubs protruded from the few feet of unpulverized ground that remained level. At the edge of the field, amputated trunks were all that remained of once proud olive trees. As he rose and moved toward the edge of the cornfield, he spotted what appeared to be fragments of animal fur scattered about the bottom of a furrow. Was it one of the rabbits? It had been so badly mangled that it was impossible to tell. Bending over, he poked at the remains with his rifle, turning each piece in search of a clue. It was the tiny piece of bright orange fur that told him that it was the little girl's dog.

Suddenly alerted by the cloud of dust rising from the road below the farm, he pinched off the lit end of the cigarette and hurriedly stuffed the unsmoked portion into his vest pocket. Once the car came to a halt, the driver jumped out and opened the rear door. An officer emerged and approached the sergeant, who was frozen in a salute. The unexpected visitor casually touched the brim of his cap with his baton, spoke briefly with the sergeant, and then slipped into the house.

Never comfortable around generals, the sergeant whistled a sigh of relief and then ambled over to where his new counterpart was gathering some of the officer's things. He looked friendly enough—pretty grimy, though. He must have been driving all day.

"Tell me," ventured the sergeant, "how is it driving for a general, especially this one?"

"Well, it was fine up till the last few days, but now he can't get close enough to the front lines. I only volunteered for this duty because I thought it would get me away from the fighting," he grumbled, snapping his head in the direction of their bullet riddled car. The sergeant offered a knowing nod.

"How about you?" he continued. "Been with the colonel long?"

"Since Russia."

The sergeant began fumbling for his half-smoked cigarette when he spotted a familiar bulge in the driver's lapel pocket and wondered how a fresh smoke would taste.

"Can you spare a cigarette?" he asked.

"Help yourself," said the driver, tossing the pack toward him.

"Thanks. Going to be with us long?"

"No. Just for tonight. The general must feel that we're not close enough to the shooting yet, so we'll be headed south first thing in the morning."

"That's a huge waste of time and gasoline," quipped the sergeant. "In a couple of days, the front will have come to us." Carefully, he lit two cigarettes and handed one to the driver, and both men inhaled deeply.

"All we need now," he quipped, "are blindfolds!"

* * *

Inside the farmhouse, there was a flurry of activity. The moment the general arrived, the colonel immediately summoned all of the local commanders to the new temporary headquarters.

"Sergeant," snapped the colonel through the open doorway, "I want all family members to get out of the house."

"When, sir?"

"Immediately"

"For how long, sir?"

"For as long as the general is here."

As the sergeant went off to implement the order, the colonel moved toward the large table around which the others had already assembled. The general was moving his finger across the large map that lay on the table.

"Here, to the south," he noted, "the Moroccans now hold the high ground and are within striking distance of Pico." His attention then shifted to the southeast. "And here we have the French and Algerians rushing up the Ausente Valley. They are also headed directly toward Pico."

"What about our flank, sir?"

"The news is even worse. Cassino is under heavy siege, and the Poles are putting relentless pressure on the abbey. Here in the south, the Americans are moving again, albeit slowly. So, gentlemen as you can see ..."

The ringing field phone atop the table cut him short. The colonel answered it and quickly handed the phone to the general.

"Yes! Good. I understand. I'll see to it immediately!" He hung up and turned to his staff.

"Gentlemen, that was Kesselring. He has informed me that he has already released a division of Panzer Grenadiers from Anzio and ordered them here. I have also been told to disengage and withdraw from both the abbey and the town of Cassino. That leaves it up to us in Pico. The enemy must be stopped, here and now!"

* * *

At the crack of dawn the next day, the family watched as the general's car sped down the hill. He was gone. They didn't know who he was, and they didn't care. They had just spent the night in the remnants of straw where the chickens once nested. They simply wanted their beds back.

U.S. Army Military History Institute
Lt. Gen. Frido von Senger und Etterlin.

CHAPTER NINE
Flight to the Caves

*If the day should come when we must go,
if some day we are compelled to leave the
scene of history, we will slam the door so hard
that the universe will shake and mankind
will stand back in stupification.*

—Joseph Goebbels, Nazi Minister of Propaganda

No sooner had the general driven off than the colonel and his sergeant emerged from the house.

"Sergeant," said the officer, "yesterday, the general ordered us to withdraw from Monte Cassino. I was just informed that this was done during the night. Unfortunately for the men in the town, the only way out was to climb up the face of the mountain. That meant leaving all of our wounded behind."

The sergeant stared into the colonel's face and said nothing.

"I have also learned that at first light, the Poles raised their colors in the abbey rubble."

"What will we do now, sir?"

"The floodgates have now been opened, and the enemy will be pouring through. We will be telling all civilians to get out, now!" he announced as he waved his arm toward the Forte family, "beginning with these people."

The sergeant then turned to face the family. "The fighting will soon be here, and this house is nothing more than a big target." His matter-of-fact tone had its intended effect. "We will be notifying the people in town," he continued, "and the colonel and I will be moving on. I trust you will do the same." This unwelcome assessment of their circumstances brought a

National Archives and Records Administration
The Prize. The abbey atop Monte Cassino a few days after the Polish raised their colors within the ruins. In the foreground stands what is left of a once-thriving forest.

The Price. This photo, taken from the abbey itself, shows the cemetery on nearby Mount Cairo, which serves as the final resting place for the more than eleven hundred Poles who lost their lives in the final assault on the mountain.

stunned silence. They all knew that this moment would come but had prayed that it wouldn't.

"Where can we go?" pleaded Rosario. "The roads are clogged with tanks and trucks, and they are constantly being bombed and strafed."

"You've answered your own question," said the sergeant. "Stay away from the roads."

As the soldier turned to leave, little Mimino, who was standing next to Maria, pointed toward the sergeant and cried, *"Maria! Guarda il porco!"*

"Look at what pig?" said the grizzled veteran as he froze in his tracks. He swirled around, and shot an angry glare at the child. He could not ignore such an insult. "Perhaps someone will remind him that I speak your language, and I don't wish to be to be called a pig." His eyes then searched out Vittoria, and he snapped, "Your son needs to be taught better manners."

"No, no, Signore Sergente," interrupted Maria, as she pointed behind where he stood, "he meant that *thing!*" As he turned toward the unexploded bomb that still lay partially buried in front of the house, his face suddenly softened. What the sergeant saw was a five-hundred-pound cylinder, roughly one foot in diameter and five and one-half feet long: a free fall bomb, designed to explode upon contact with the ground. He could almost understand how the less structured mind of a six-year-old might think of it as a pig. "That's one more reason for you to leave as quickly as possible," he noted. "Just because that *thing* didn't go off, doesn't mean that it won't. If and when it ever explodes, it will take your house with it, along with anyone unfortunate enough to be inside. And furthermore ..." His lecture was cut short by an impatient grunt from the colonel, who had been waiting in the sidecar. "I am sorry, but we must leave immediately, and so should you."

"Arrivederci," he added. Then, after touching his cap, he moved toward the waiting motorcycle.

"Arrivederci," whispered Maria Civita, "and good riddance."

* * *

In and around Pico, tanks and gun emplacements punctuated the landscape. At the Forte farm, panic mounted as the angry sounds of rifle and mortar fire could now be heard in the distance. There was no time to unearth the foodstuffs that they had so carefully hidden. They had little more than one or two days provisions on hand, but it would have to do. Maria Civita bundled up a few cooking utensils, along with some soap and matches. Attilio fetched firewood and some skins of water from the well, while Rosario gathered up a few knives, a hatchet, a hammer, and whatever other tools might be needed for survival. Vittoria and the grandparents collected clothing and bedding and then tied them into bundles with rawhide.

Meanwhile, Maria, Sabetta, and Mimino set about the task of burying what was left of Dog. After finding a small spot that hadn't been churned up by bombs, they dug a modest hole and scooped the remnants of hair and bone into it with a shovel. Once they had refilled the hole and troweled it over with the back of the shovel, Maria and Sabetta stood looking down at the tiny grave. Burying what was left of Dog had been a heart-wrenching experience. Unlike the other farm animals, his remarkable talent and unquestioning loyalty had endeared him to the children. *Why is everybody trying to kill us?* Maria asked silently. The futility of the question nagged at her eight-year-old mind. Sabetta's thoughts, however, were elsewhere.

"Are we supposed to say a prayer or something?" she asked.

"I don't know. Do dogs go to heaven?"

"I never heard the grown-ups say anything about that."

"Just in case, it probably wouldn't hurt if we—"

The makeshift service was suddenly interrupted by Vittoria's screams. The two girls looked up to where she stood on the balcony, leaning over the railing with outstretched arms, shouting, "Mimino! Mimino! Somebody get him! Oh God, please get him out of there!" All the while the girls had been occupied with Dog's internment, Mimino had wandered over to play at the spot in front of the house where the unexploded bomb lay, half buried in the ground. Fueled by his mother's screams, the two girls raced to where the six-year-old now sat atop the bomb, straddling it with both legs and bouncing cheerfully up and down, shouting, "Come on, pig. Move, pig." Standing on either side of him, they grabbed him and carefully slid him down his imaginary mount. "Mimino," scolded Maria, "what's the matter with you. Are you crazy?"

"Let go," he complained. "That's my pig."

"It's not a pig so, stop calling it that. It's a bomb, and it can kill us all."

"It's a pig."

"For the last time, it's not a pig. Look up on the balcony. You've frightened your mother half to death. Promise you'll never go near that thing again."

Having arrived at this somewhat shaky truce with the boy, the two friends agreed to meet tomorrow and said good-bye. Maria, with Mimino in tow, turned back toward the house.

* * *

The once distant gunfire was now much closer, and it had become abundantly clear that the family must leave immediately. From a friend, Rosario learned of some empty caves in the mountains approximately two kilometers from the farm, where many people were finding refuge. After some exploratory work, he discovered there were enough caves to also harbor his sister, Concetta, along with her family. So, armed with the meager possessions they had been able to assemble, the family gathered in front of the house and prepared to leave.

"There," said Maria Civita, as she gingerly placed the load on Maria's head. "Is that too heavy for you?"

The child stiffened slightly and shifted the load. "How much does it weigh?" she asked.

"About thirty pounds."

"I'll be all right, Mamma."

"Let's get going," interrupted Rosario as he turned to take a final inventory of the disenfranchised caravan. "Wait! Where's Nonna?"

"I last saw her sitting at the table in the kitchen," said Vittoria.

Rosario rushed back into the house, and an exchange of muddled shouting came from the open doorway. When it stopped, a bewildered Rosario emerged and announced, "*Pazza*. She's absolutely crazy."

"What do you mean?" asked Attilio.

"She's not going anywhere."

"She what?"

"She told me that she's spent her entire life on this farm, and no army in the world could ever force her to leave."

"But if she stays, she'll be killed."

"Of course she will, but there's no talking to her. She simply sits there, shouting, 'Go! Go! Just leave me alone.' So I gave her a half loaf of bread and told her how to get to the caves just in case she changes her mind. I only hope that hunger will succeed where logic has failed. Let's go. She's not going to leave, and if we stay any longer, we'll all be killed along with her."

"Stubbornness is the curse of old age," quipped Maria Civita as she straightened the load on her head. Rosario then led the tiny procession across the ruined fields, toward the mountains. As they moved along, little Maria's thoughts returned to her last meeting with Sabetta. They had just buried Dog and lifted Mimino from the bomb. Since then, everything had happened so quickly. First, the colonel had left the house, and suddenly, they were all going to live in some caves. It was the first time the girls had been separated, and she missed her dear friend already. Perhaps Sabetta's family would be coming to the caves also?

*   *   *

Immediately after they left, low-flying light bombers began smashing the nearby German positions with deadly precision. Sabetta's parents realized that they would never survive another air raid if they remained in their little shack, so, they decided to seek shelter with the Fortes. Surely if they asked, the family would let them in. They raced up to the farmhouse, only to find it empty. Sabetta's father shot a glance down the narrow hall and spotted the stairway leading up to the second floor. "Quickly," he barked, "everyone under the stairs." Seconds later, Sabetta, along with her parents and older sister, raced down the hallway and huddled as best they could behind the partially open staircase. Sabetta, being the smallest, was the last to reach the relative safety beneath the staircase and was positioned at the outer edge of the group. Upstairs, unbeknown to them, Nonna lay trembling beneath her bed.

No sooner had Sabetta's family secured themselves than the bombing resumed. Once again, the target was the German anti-aircraft guns at the base of the hill. In their rush to safety, however, someone in the family had left the large front door slightly ajar. It was a mere slit of an opening, but it was all that was needed for the tiny bomb fragment to fly through the crack and bury itself in the back of Sabetta's head. Her lifeless body slumped silently backward into a small pool of blood.

* * *

Nothing could have prepared the Fortes for the miserable life that awaited them in the caves. Sleep was only possible when brought on by complete exhaustion. What little water they had was rationed exclusively for drinking, and any notion of personal hygiene was quickly abandoned. Terrorized by the nearby gunfire, they huddled together in their self-imposed prison, never venturing far from the mouth of the cave, except for an occasional visit to the nearby open ditch that served as a communal latrine. By noon of the second day, what little food they had managed to bring was nearly gone, and Rosario, armed with an empty sack, stood at the edge of the cave, staring down the side of the mountain.

"What do you think, Mamma? Should I risk going back for Nonna?"

"She's probably dead by now."

"Maybe so, but if not, she might just be hungry enough to come back with me; anyway, I might be able to scavenge something along the way."

"All right, go ... go! But please, be careful."

When Rosario arrived at the farm, he was stunned by what he saw. Every window on the house had been blown away, and the exterior walls were ravaged by shrapnel. The chickens and sheep were gone. Only the horse remained, rotting in the field. Desperately, he clawed away at the edges of the haystack. There, by some miracle, he found two eggs. Not much, but they would have to do. As he turned the corner of the house, he came upon a pair of German soldiers who were in the process of completing Sabetta's makeshift grave. One knelt, nervously holding a small wooden cross, while the other drove it into the ground with the face of a shovel. The lettering on the cross read *"Forte, ragazzina"*—Forte, little girl. He had seen them both before. They were two of the colonel's men who had been stationed at the base of the hill. The one with the shovel spoke first. "Signore Forte, we are sorry about your little sister. We found her dead beneath the stairs, and if you will tell us her first name, we'll mark it on the cross also."

"That's impossible!"gasped Rosario. "My sister is with the rest of my family in the mountains."

"But we thought since we found her inside your house that ..."

"Never mind," interrupted the second soldier. "We're done here." And with their business finished, they turned and started down the hill. Rosario stood for a moment, staring at them. Then his puzzled gaze shifted down toward the little cross. *It certainly wasn't Maria, but who could it be?* No matter. That would have to wait inasmuch as he had food to fetch and a grandmother to find. He raced to the front of the building and leaned into the open doorway. "Nonna," he yelled, "Nonna, are you in there? Nonna ... Nonna!" Nothing! Where could she have gone? Suddenly, rifle shots broke out at the base of the hill, and the two German soldiers dropped to the ground and began firing at some figures in the distance. With or without his grandmother, he couldn't wait around any longer. As he raced toward the safety of the hedgerow at the edge of the farm, he spotted an injured rabbit that had limped into the brush. Slowed by the wound, it quickly ended up in Rosario's sack. "One small rabbit and two eggs," he mused, "won't go very far." He glanced back to where the dead horse lay and then disappeared into the hedgerow.

In the upstairs window, a hand, leathered by many Italian suns, pulled the tattered drape aside. This made it easier for the old woman to see her grandson place something in his sack and slip into the brush.

CHAPTER TEN
War Comes to Pico

Indeed, many dogs surround me.
A pack of evildoers closes in
upon me; they have pierced
my hands and feet; I can count all my bones.

Psalm 22: 17–18

The battle for Pico had begun. The Gustav Line had been smashed, and most of *La Ciociara* lay in smoldering ruins. Von Senger was now receiving bad news on an hourly basis. The Algerians and French had broken into the orchards on the outskirts of town, and the Moroccans now held the Pico-Itri road. In addition to these losses, artillery from God-knows-where was raining onto his now compacted force. His greatest fear, however, came from the news that Kesselring's belated replacements had been unable to contain the American advance along the coast. If they weren't stopped, they could easily outflank him and annihilate his entire command. He was rapidly losing his tactical options.

The following day, things continued to unravel. Von Senger was forced to withdraw from the outskirts of town. This meant that the handful of Picanos who chose to remain in their homes would pay dearly for their decision. Artillery from both sides slammed into Pico indiscriminately, killing scores in their homes as walls and ceilings came crashing down upon them. Still others died in a belated attempt to flee along the roadways. The fighting became so intense that control of the streets would shift from hour to hour throughout the day. The dead and the dying lay where they fell.

Von Senger was now told that the Americans to his south were presently in position to turn his left flank and cut off his retreat. Unable to bring in reinforcements and unable to make do with what he had, he realized the situation was hopeless. To compound the problem, the rain had let up and he was once again being pounded from the air.

* * *

It was midday, and from her upstairs bedroom, Nonna could hear the crack of rifles nearby, along with the sporadic chatter of machine gun fire. As the afternoon light glistened from shattered window panes, she could also see flashes from weapons on either side of the corn field. There were soldiers moving about, jockeying for position, some firing from where they crouched, others standing behind trees for protection. If one fell, another rose quickly to take his place. The firefight was so close that the stench from spent gunpowder lingered just below her window. At the bottom of the hill, hatchways on tanks slammed shut as they ground their way up the hill, toward the cornfield.

She now realized that it had all been a terrible mistake. To stay meant to die. She must get out, now! *They can have the farm.* Acting from an unconscious reflex, she rolled up a blanket, tucked it under her arm, and rushed down the staircase, into the yard. It had begun to rain. Impervious to the line of battle, she stepped deliberately out into the mud and raced toward the long hedgerow at the far end of the cornfield. The impact from bullets suddenly spit mud upwards in front of her path. Frozen in place, she dropped the roll, fell to her knees, and pressed the palms of her hands together. *"Santa Maria, Madre di Dio ..."* The deadly geysers came even closer.

To her left, a man's voice shouted, and the shooting from that side suddenly stopped. Seconds later, a voice to her right also barked out, and the cornfield suddenly fell silent. From either side of the field, eyes stared out from faces blackened by combat and intent on the work of killing. She looked to either side of the field. Men were shouting and motioning for her to get up and run. What was happening? Would she be shot the moment she rose to her feet? It no longer mattered. The old woman rose carefully, glanced to either side, picked up her mud-soaked blanket, and darted forward again. Twice, her seventy-year-old body fell, and twice it rose. *Click!*

Click! On either side of the field, rifle bolts were being slammed into position. Numbed and exhausted, she finally stumbled forward into the safety of the thicket. As quickly as it had stopped, the gunfire once again resumed its full fury. The pounding in her chest made it almost impossible to breath. Grabbing onto what was left of a nearby sapling, she struggled to her feet and looked down, only to discover that the suction created by running through the mud had pulled off both her *cioci*. She knew of no earthly reason she should still be alive. Could it be that for one magnificent moment, the blackened faces along the edges of the field recognized the importance of a single human life? She glanced back into what had once again become no-man's-land, shook her head, and stumbled barefoot in the general direction of the caves.

Meanwhile, in those very caves, the continuous rain had downgraded living conditions from miserable to wretched. Water now flooded the floor of the cave, turning it into an unforgiving slime that saturated the family's clothing and provisions. It was impossible to start a fire. Nearly out of food and unable to sleep, they waited helplessly as the sound and smell of battle drifted ever closer. Only out of desperation did anyone venture as far as the open cesspool. Her face drained of hope, Maria Civita looked skyward and complained loudly to whoever might be listening that she wasn't going to feed raw rabbit to her family—at least, not yet! As they set out pots and containers to collect the precious rainwater, little Maria quipped, "It's not really so bad, Mamma."

"How can you say a thing like that?"

"Because when it rains, they don't drop bombs on us."

*   *   *

By any standard, it wasn't much of a rabbit; nevertheless, Rosario was thankful for it. *One piece for everyone*, he mused as he carefully placed each bite-sized share onto the little section of chicken-wire fencing that he had fashioned into a grill. Meanwhile, his mother assembled the legs of a metal tripod that she had brought from the farmhouse hearth and hung a small kettle in its center. For his part, Attilio had spent most of the morning chopping kindling from several small pieces of wood planking. This was all that was left of the henhouse. The clearing skies meant that they would now be able to light a fire. Maria and Mimino, as instructed, had each fetched a pail of rainwater and emptied it into the kettle. Holding the empty containers, they waited patiently for further instructions. "Now, I want both of you to fill your pails with grass," Maria Civita intoned, "but stay away from the latrine and don't bring back any roots, just the green part." As they scurried off, she carefully began arranging Attilio's hard-earned kindling beneath the kettle.

The water had just come to a boil when the children returned with their treasure. The entire family gathered around and watched as Maria Civita slid Rosario's improvised grill onto the fire. She then culled a handful of cornmeal from a nearby sack and dropped it into the boiling water. Hungry eyes locked onto her as she turned toward the children, took their pails, and emptied the grass into the kettle. Slowly stirring the concoction, she looked into the drawn faces of the hungry gathering. Unnoticed, she leaned toward Vittoria and whispered her dark secret: "This is the last of the cornmeal!"

* * *

Early on the third day of battle, Von Senger's men continued to fall back from the Allied onslaught. As they retreated through the nearby foothills, a handful of German stragglers stumbled into the cave area occupied by various families and took up temporary shelter. To most of the community of Italian refugees, their presence in the caves was an ominous sign—but not to Vittoria. Knowing that they all faced starvation, she saw the soldiers as a possible source of food. In the hope of scavenging some scraps, she inched toward the cave in which the Germans were hiding. Once there, she noticed a small open sack containing what appeared to be about a pound of grain. *A miracle*, she thought as she reached out toward the tiny promise of survival. Suddenly, a hand clamped around her wrist, jerking it back. Startled, she looked up into the darkened face of a soldier. His other hand held a bayonet, which was tracing a tiny circle not more than three inches from her throat.

"No, *signora*," he growled.

She pulled away, only to be surprised by the release of his grip.
"You need?"His Italian was barely passable.
"Yes."
"Give two eggs."
Two eggs? He was willing to trade the grain for two eggs?
The terms for barter were not negotiable, so he grabbed the sack and waved her away with the tip of his bayonet. It was obvious that the grain would go much further than a couple of eggs, so she hurried back to Rosario, told him of the offer, and returned to the soldier with the two eggs her brother-in-law had found in the haystack earlier. True to his word, the soldier honored the agreement. It wasn't much to divide up among the entire family, but at least it was something.

* * *

Meanwhile, Von Senger received some incredibly good news. The American commander to his south had squandered a golden opportunity. He had failed to move against Von Senger's flank and provided the Germans with an avenue of escape. Von Senger immediately began to withdraw what was left of it northward toward Ceprano. Some units continued to resist as savage fighting continued in the cemetery atop the hill, where ground changed hands several times during the day. As night fell, however, all German forces inside Pico had disengaged and moved out. What was left of the little *paesa* was now firmly in Allied hands. The mind-numbing silence that followed evoked a collective sigh of relief from the cave people. The scourge of Pico was finally over ... or so it seemed.

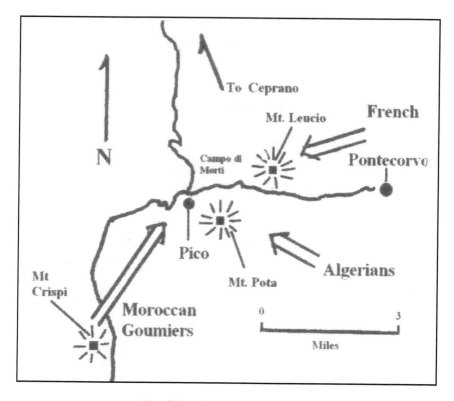

The fall of Pico: May 20–23.

CHAPTER ELEVEN
The Moment of Truth

There's no good news tonight!

At precisely 6:30 PM, the rasp from the clack horn announced the arrival of lunch hour. Seconds later, the factory whined into silence as men peeled off their shop aprons and lined up to punch out. One by one, they filed into the large, windowless lunch room escorted by the acrid smell of cutting oil and spent welding rods. Some began dealing cards while others unfolded newspapers or gathered in small groups. As usual, Domenico took a seat next to an acorn-shaped radio at the end of a long lunch table. He preferred working the second shift for a couple of reasons. First, it provided him with a much-needed night-pay bonus, and second, it enabled him to spend the precious daylight hours with his bees and his garden. It was an added convenience that the timing of the lunch break coincided nicely with the evening radio news.

He, along with four other men on this shift, had formed an informal supper club. On each day of the week, they took turns preparing sandwiches to share in their little group. Today, Wednesday, was Domenico's turn. The others looked forward to the middle of the week because they knew from experience he would bring something, well, *different*. As was their custom, the first three sat down across from Domenico, took their sandwiches from his paper bag, and bit in.

"Oh. This is great!" said one.

"Yeah," chimed another, "you outdid yourself tonight."

As Domenico peeled the wax paper from his own sandwich, the last member of the club, a young sweeper they called Four-F, struggled onto the bench next to him. Four-F was a pleasant fellow in his mid-twenties who suffered from a club foot. He was extremely self-conscious of his handicap and didn't much care for his nickname, but, such being the nature of blue-collar camaraderie, the louder he protested, the more it stuck.

"Well, my friend," he grinned, "what grand adventure is on the menu tonight?"

"Here," said Domenico, sliding the bag over to him, *"mangia!"*

Four-F tore the paper off and quickly chomped down on his newly acquired prize.

"Yum," he grinned. "This is really good. What's in it?"

Heads suddenly turned up from their card games and eyes peeked out over the tops of newspapers.

"Burdocks," grunted Domenico.

"Come on, what's in it?"

"Burdocks."

"You mean those prickly little things that always stick to your socks and pant cuffs?"

"You like?"

"Oh God! Are those things inside of me? They'll prickle me apart. I'm gonna die for sure!"

"Now you no like?"

Four-F jumped to his feet, spit the half-chewed remnants onto the floor, and clutched at his throat as though he were dangling from the end of a lynch rope. Bad leg and all, he raced out the lunchroom door toward a waiting water fountain. Cards and newspapers dropped to the floor as the room erupted in laughter. A voice from in back shouted, "Hey, Domenico, that was great, but now that he's gone, tell us what was *really* in those sandwiches?"

"*Cardo*. You just peel away the skin from the stalk and eat what's inside."

"Cardo, huh? What does that mean in English?"

"Burdocks."

Suddenly subdued by this newfound knowledge, the remaining members of the supper club sat in stunned silence and lifted the corners of their bread. Unaware that this posed a problem, Domenico brushed some crumbs onto the floor, pulled a watch from his pocket, and turned on the radio.

"Good evening from the newsroom," snapped the baritone voice. "In Washington today, President Roosevelt entered the Naval

Medical Center in Bethesda, Maryland, for his annual checkup. This is being hailed by some political observers as a first step in his expected run for reelection this Fall."

"He's a cinch to win," came a voice from behind a newspaper.

"Yeah. Nobody's going to beat him," nodded another.

"Elsewhere," continued the announcer, "Secretary of the Navy James Forrestal, while speaking at New York's Waldorf Astoria, noted that navy sea and air power will likely be our primary source of international strength in the years to come. News from the front after this word from the makers of ..."

As if on cue, Four-F, red-faced and clinging to his collar with both hands, stumbled back into the room.

"Hey, Four-F," came a voice from the corner, "go see the company nurse. Maybe she knows the cure for *prickly poison*." They all roared.

"Domenico," chimed another, "see if he wants to take a drag on your pipe, too." They roared even louder. Four-F slumped back into his seat and tore at a piece of bread with his teeth.

"Now, news from the front," crackled the voice on the radio. "Brigadier General Frank Merrill has rejoined his Marauders as they continue to grind their way through northern Burma, toward the Japanese-held Myitkyina air field." The men stopped playing cards and put down their newspapers. All eyes locked on the radio as the voice continued, "In the Mediterranean Theater, the Germans are now in full retreat along the Gustav Line as American and British forces are rapidly advancing along both coastlines. The Germans, meanwhile, continued their 'scorched earth' policy by burning Gaeta to the ground before abandoning it. Advancing American forces are reported to have reached the coastal town only to find it completely engulfed in flames." Domenico's lower lip began to quiver. "Meanwhile, in the center, the French Expeditionary Corps, which includes both Algerian and Moroccan elements, has been involved in a savage battle against stubborn German resistance in and around the tiny village of Pico, roughly ten miles north of the now burning Gaeta. There are reports of both heavy civilian and military casualties in the three-day battle just ended. Elsewhere in the news, Axis Sally is at it again. With the invasion of Europe soon to take place, from her perch in Berlin, she ..."

In an awkward attempt to shut off the radio, Domenico's trembling hand fell onto the table. Four-F gently steadied him with one hand and then reached out with the other and snapped the dial. All faces turned downward in awkward silence as Domenico sat trembling in his private hell—a silence that would be unceremoniously shattered by the uncaring clack horn as it barked them all back to work.

CHAPTER TWELVE
The Scourge of the Goumiers

You must not lose faith in humanity.
Humanity is an ocean: if a few drops of
the ocean are dirty, the ocean does not
become dirty.

—Mahatma Gandhi

It had taken three full days to destroy Pico. Back at the caves, the German stragglers had been captured and the sounds of war had vanished. Emboldened by the relative silence and driven by hunger, Rosario chanced a second return to the farm in the hope of unearthing some of the buried food. Standing in front of the house, he was totally unprepared for the panorama of destruction that unfolded before him. Unlike the tiny streets in the town, the soft, rolling hills around the farm provided a more appropriate arena for tank warfare. Everywhere he had buried food, the land had been churned and compacted by tank tracks from the shattered steel hulks that now smoldered silently in the fields. In the ravine, a pall of dirty gray smoke lingered over the spot where the colonel's anti-aircraft once lay in wait.

He knew he must hurry. He raced into the house and down the narrow corridor to where he had hidden the shovel. It was gone! Nothing remained but a small puddle of dried blood. *The soldiers digging the grave*—they had been using *his* shovel. He dashed from the house and squinted out into the smog. Something moved! A booted foot appeared in the distance, then a long, striped robe. Through the fog, he could hear high-pitched voices, and they were coming closer. He slipped back into the hedgerow. There were ten or twelve of them. They were soldiers, all right, but not like any he had ever seen before. In addition to their striped robes, some wore what appeared to be dark turbans, while others wore World-War-I-style helmets. Their leathery, bearded faces told him that they were definitely not Americans. He crouched lower and watched as they approached the front of the farmhouse. He was closer than he cared to be. *They're out of luck if they think there is anything of value left in there.* No sooner had that thought formed than two of them pounded the pins out of the hinges, stripped the large wooden front door from its frame, and began smashing it to pieces. Others scrambled into the house, dragged the wooden table and chairs from the kitchen, and proceeded to smash them, as well. They then led a couple of mules up the hill and loaded them with the bundled wood remnants. Apparently satisfied, they turned and started moving down the hill. As the odd-looking procession wandered away, one of the soldiers suddenly peeled his rifle from his shoulder and spun around, facing Rosario's general direction. Blood pounded through his temples. Had he moved? Had he made a sound? A voice crackled out from one of the other mule skinners. The soldier then turned away, slung the rifle back onto his shoulder, and followed the others down the hill.

The family still needed food and a shovel. If Rosario were going to find either, he would have to get closer to town. Carefully, he moved in that direction, avoiding any well-traveled roads or pathways. Upon reaching the edge of town, he was appalled by what he saw. The narrow cobblestone streets where Maria had once frolicked in a sea of flowers now ran red with blood. It appeared that much of the combat had been in close quarters. Rubble littered the streets, and what buildings remained were no more than roofless, windowless shells. He was close enough to hear the voices of soldiers laboring to clear the rubble from streets. They were French. In the distance, he could also hear the sound of artillery coming from the general direction of Ceprano.

It was clear to him that there was nothing of value in the village. As he moved farther into the outskirts, he arrived at the cemetery. It had fared no better. The bullet-riddled mausoleum walls now surrounded the remains of the newly dead. Rosario observed from a distance as German prisoners stacked bodies onto waiting trucks under the watchful eyes of their captors. In the center of

the cemetery stood the roofless shell of the tiny church of Sant'
Antonino, its sanctuary buried under fallen rubble. He moved along
the crest and spotted the smoldering remains of a pillbox, its giant
gun pointing skyward as if in mock salute to its dead occupants. He
had seen enough. There was nothing for him to bring back to the
caves. It was time to get back to his family. Upon reaching a small
back road just outside of town, he saw an old man bent over with his
hands cupped atop his knees, gasping for air. After several labored
breaths, he straightened, looked anxiously over his shoulder, and
began stumbling forward. Rosario recognized him at once. It was
Enrico, the owner of a small coffee shop in town where he had
occasionally played cards. He was a jolly sort, always mingling with
the players, endlessly kibitzing—the first to groan over a missed play
and the loudest to roar when a trump came crashing down on one
of the *briscola* tables.

His once glowing eyes now stared aimlessly into space, the levity
in his face replaced by hardened fear.

"Enrico," shouted Rosario. There was no answer.

"Enrico!" The old man stopped, his glazed eyes searching for a
familiar face.

"Is that you, Rosario?"

"*Si,* Enrico. Are you all right?"

"All right? I'll never be all right again."

"You're not making any sense."

"*Animali ... animali,*" he muttered as he turned and pointed a
trembling finger back toward the town. "They're tearing Pico apart,
stone by stone."

"Animals? You're talking crazy. What's happened?"

"When the fighting stopped, some of us came back to town to
see what, if anything, was left."

"And?"

"Do you remember Tino, the fellow who owns the shop next to
my place?"

"Of course; everyone knows him."

"Well, when I last saw him, they had dragged him out into the
street and cut him down with their knives."

"Why? What did he do?"

"Nothing. They wanted his woman."

"*Madre di Dio.*"

The old man's voice thickened. "There must have been ten or twenty of them," he went on, "lined up at the front door, waiting for a turn at her. Imagine ... there he was, lying in the street, eyes open but seeing nothing."

"Why would the Americans do a thing like that?"

"Americans? These men are not Americans. They are *Marocchini.*"

Rosario knew nothing of Moroccans. "Were they wearing striped robes?"

"*Si,*" the old man gasped. "They looted everything and then smashed our furniture into firewood."

That explained it.

"Enrico," Rosario pleaded, "come with me. I know a place where you'll be safe."

"*Grazia,* but I have twelve- and fourteen-year-old granddaughters at home. I must get them and bring them with me."

"Very well, then. Let me at least show you where this place is." Rosario squatted and traced a crude map into the dirt with his finger. "Here is our farm, and over here are the caves. Now, for God's sake, hurry! These *Marocchini* are all around us."

* * *

No sooner had he returned to the girls than Enrico found the soldiers to be everywhere. It would be impossible to get through to the caves, and after what he had witnessed in town, he knew what to expect. With sweat rolling into his eyes, he hid in the darkness next to the open doorway of his home. An old pickax leaned against the wall beside him. It wouldn't be enough, but it was all he had.

"Nonno," cried one of the girls, "can we come out now?"

"*Silenzio,*" he snapped. "I don't want to hear another word from either of you."

He glanced back at the stones that he had piled up in front of the large brick oven, inside which the two girls lay in hiding.

He could see the soldiers now. There were ten or fifteen of them. They were about thirty yards away.

He propped himself against the wall and looked back toward the pile of stones. "I want you two to remain very still."

After wiping the palm of his hands against his shirt, he lifted the pickax in a slow, determined motion. With one hand at the bottom and the other near its head, he spun the handle so that the pick end pointed forward. His trembling hands made it hard to grip.

Suddenly, the first one appeared in the doorway. The old man lunged forward, and in one fluid motion, skewered the soldier's chest. The impact drove the soldier backwards, pulling Enrico with him. Rage now replaced fear as he stumbled forward through the doorway, jerking at the handle to pull it free. It finally came loose, but it was too late. Goumier knives made short work of him. Mercifully, he never heard their screams as the two girls were being dragged from the oven.

National Archives and Records Administration
May 25, 1944, a French soldier examines the remains of a chapel in the village of Pico.

National Archives and Records Administration
Soldiers clear the rubble from the streets of Pico after the battle
had moved on.

*   *   *

It had been two days since the fall of Pico. Although the mist of battle had been burned away by the Italian sun, an ominous silence now hung over the cave people. There were stories about murder, rape, and looting in town. There were also rumors that the *Marocchini* had begun plundering some of the nearby caves. A cook pot and a handful of tools were pitiful weapons; even the shovel was now gone.

From his perch on the stone ridge overlooking the cave, Attilio cried out, "Mamma, I can see them. They are coming, and they have rifles." The snap of crackling brush accompanied by strange-sounding voices confirmed their approach. Attilio slid quickly down next to the mouth of the cave. Maria Civita rose to her feet and, with trembling hands, grabbed Maria's arm and pulled her in the direction of the open latrine. No matter how revolting the thought, it must be done—now! When they arrived at the edge of the cesspool, several women from nearby caves were already standing ankle deep in the filth, gagging and sobbing as they rubbed it onto themselves.

"Child," she pleaded, "listen carefully. We must do the same."

"Why, Mamma?"

How could she explain rape to an eight-year-old?

"There's no time! Here, take my hand and we'll go in together." She began pulling her daughter forward.

"*Aspetta, Signora, aspetta!*" came the voice from directly behind her. "*Sono Francese!*"

French? Did he say he was French?

She spun to face him. He was no more than thirty feet away, and although he wasn't dressed like the soldiers Rosario described, it could still be some kind of trick.

"*Francese?*"

"*Si, Signora.*"

"Why should I believe you? You're probably in with those other men."

"Those men have been ordered on ahead. They will not be coming back." His voice was soft but firm. "Believe me. You have nothing more to fear."

She wanted desperately to believe him, but this might be the last chance they had to save themselves. "Do you know my Pappa?" This time the voice came from little Maria.

"What?"

"His name is Domenico Forte and he lives in America. Is that far from France?"

"Yes, it is," grinned the soldier, "and America is a very big place."

Perhaps it was the sincerity in his smile or the softness of his voice; either way, Maria Civita gently released her grip on the eight-year-old's hand.

* * *

The family was told to stay in the middle of the road as they straggled back toward Pico. Long columns of soldiers going in the opposite direction walked expressionlessly on either side of them. It was the same road that crossed the bottom of the hill near the farmhouse. Still carrying her possessions atop her head, little Maria glanced upward at what remained of their home. The windowless exterior of the house had been badly scared, and the colonel's sign now hung diagonally across the empty doorway. In its place, other signs now dotted the fields along side of the road, proclaiming, "Attenzione, Pericolo—Campo Minato!"

"Rosario," she asked, "what is a *Campo Minato* and why do the signs say it's dangerous?"

"It's a mine field," he answered. "It's a place where they bury bombs in the ground, and if you step on one, it will blow you to pieces. This is why they won't let us return to our home."

"Oh."

As they continued on down the road, she again looked back toward the farm. The bloated carcass of the horse still lay rotting in the field, and Mimino's "pig" remained half buried in the mud near the front of the house. A few feet away stood a little makeshift cross. *What could that mean?* she wondered. No matter; she would ask Sabetta when they next met.

CHAPTER THIRTEEN
Some Brief Military Notes

"How would I like to be remembered?
I don't know if I really care about being
remembered. I just want to be known
while I am here. That's enough.
I didn't like history anyway."

— Interviewee to Studs Terkel [3]

Although not previously mentioned by name, General Mark Clark was the American general who failed to cut off Von Senger's retreat immediately after the fall of Pico. In what may well have been the most controversial decision of the Italian campaign, Clark, ignoring his orders, elected instead to turn his army north toward Rome. It was reported that Clark, long suspicious of British intentions, saw the liberation of the Eternal City as *his* prize, along with the attendant photo ops and headlines. Whatever the reason, Von Senger was no fool. Handed this opportunity, he beat a hasty retreat northward, where he would hold out until the final days of the war. In a caustic footnote to history, Clark's triumphant entry into Rome would be unceremoniously pushed from international headlines on June 6 by a much larger event known as D-Day.

Clark would go on to succeed General Matthew B. Ridgeway as supreme commander of all Allied forces involved in the Korean War. Upon his retirement from the army, he would serve for several years as president of the Citadel, a military college in South Carolina. He died in 1984 at the age of eighty-eight. He would be the last of the military personalities involved in the Italian campaign.

---

3   From *Working* by Studs Terkel. New York: Avon Books. Copyright © 1974 Studs Terkel. Reprinted by permission of Donadio & Olson, Inc.

*   *   *

On March 23, 1944, members of an Italian underground group known as the *Gruppii di Azioni Patriottica* (Patriotic Action Group) concealed an explosive device on the Via Rosella in Rome and detonated it just as a column of German soldiers marched by. Thirty-three soldiers died in the blast. An infuriated Hitler ordered the immediate execution of ten Italian citizens for every German soldier killed. His orders were carried out the following day by S.S. troops as over three hundred and thirty civilians were marched into the Ardeatine Caves of Rome and shot. This event would seal the fate of Field Marshal Albert Kesselring forever. At war's end, he was imprisoned in Germany and charged with war crimes inasmuch as the atrocities in the Ardeatine Caves were committed by troops under his command.

He was then returned to Italy to stand trial. His defense attorneys argued that the S.S. troops who committed the atrocities had acted independently of Kesselring. The prosecution, however, proved that Berlin had given him complete authority to deal with anti-partisan uprisings. His fierce loyalty to Hitler further compounded his problem, and a British tribunal promptly convicted him. He was sentenced to be hanged. Fortunately for Kesselring, capital punishment was not permitted under Italian law, and his sentence was subsequently commuted to life imprisonment. Many prominent military and political figures of the day eventually argued that the S.S. troops who had committed the atrocities in the Ardeatine Caves were only nominally under his command. They were a runaway extension of Hitler's Nazi Party. As a result of this reasoning, the now ailing Kesselring was released from prison and allowed to return to his home in Germany.

The once rising star in the German army, who very nearly turned away the Allied amphibious landing at Salerno, died quietly at home in Bad Nauheim, West Germany, on July 16, 1960, at age seventy-five. His legacy would be forever clouded by a blind obedience to one of the worst despots the world has ever known.

*   *   *

Immediately after surrendering the German armies in Italy, General Frido von Senger und Etterlin was taken prisoner in Triente, Italy. Probably the only German general at the time to have attended Oxford, he was released from prison after it was determined that he was never connected to any atrocities which occurred in Italy. Upon his release, he was allowed to return home to Germany. On January 4, 1967, Von Senger, who was probably Kesselring's most able commander and the man singularly responsible for the German stand at Pico, died at his home in Freiburg, Germany, nestled in the midst of the Black forest—the very place where the Moroccan *Goumiers* had ended their advance through Europe at war's end.

*   *   *

Less than two months after the fall of Pico, the marauding Goumiers launched an amphibious assault on the tiny island of Elba. Within two days, the attacking Moroccans crushed the German defenders, and their victory, true to form, was followed by yet another siege of looting.

Inasmuch as the Moroccan Goumiers were an integral part of General Juin's French Expeditionary Corps, he was arguably, the highest military figure connected to the atrocities they committed. Born in Algeria in 1888, Juin served in the French army during World War I, where he lost the use of his right arm in combat. In the early days of World War II, he was captured and released by the German armies shortly after their successful conquest of France.

By the time his FEC reached Italy, the Goumiers had already gained notoriety for their ruthless treatment of prisoners and civilians. On the surface, it would appear that Juin was oblivious to their conduct. History, however, tells us that he was anything but an armchair general and could frequently be found in the middle of front line combat. It is hardly surprising, therefore, that there has been considerable speculation concerning his knowledge of, and responsibility for, the deportment of his troops. This ambiguity was further fueled by his importation of Moroccan women as camp followers, in order to satisfy the insatiable needs of his Goumiers.

Juin would eventually share in the spoils of victory at the end of the war. With his Goumiers long since disbanded and returned home, he was to be awarded the position of president general of Morocco. His presidency would usher in a long period of unrest, as Colonial France was about to collapse under its own weight.

In 1964, French General Alphonse Juin died in Paris at age seventy-five. Had Germany won the war, he might well have stood in the prisoner's dock instead of Kesselring. Fortunately for Juin, that is not how history played out. His precise level of responsibility for the actions of his Goumiers may never be known, and his death appears to have closed the book on one of the darkest incidents of the Second World War.

*   *   *

French military records indicate that shortly after the atrocities that occurred in the province of Frosinone, French officers were able to regain control of their troops. Many Goumiers were summarily executed in the field, while others were tried at courts-martial and sentenced to long prison terms. The number of cases disposed of at the time was less than one hundred. On the other hand, although the total number of atrocities that occurred may never be known, some estimates place the number of women violated as high as two thousand, along with eight hundred related killings. If this number is anywhere near accurate, the disciplinary action taken would appear to be extremely disproportionate to the attendant crimes.

In spite of their well-earned stigma as brigands, the final year of the war would see the Goumiers continue on as part of the Allied assault that swept through western and central Europe. Their final days of battle would end in the spring of 1945, in the Black Forest of southern Germany. Juin's twelve-thousand-man band of mountain fighters suffered over eight thousand casualties, of which one thousand six hundred and twenty-five were killed in action.

*   *   *

Neither the colonel nor his sergeant were ever seen or heard from again. It is unknown whether or not they survived the war, let alone the battle for Pico. They will forever remain nameless.

CHAPTER FOURTEEN
A Promise Fulfilled: 1947

*It is a peculiarity of man that he can only
live by looking to the future ... and this is
his salvation in the most difficult moment of
his existence.*

—Victor Frankl [4]

Long after war's end, the people of the Liri Valley would continue to be killed or maimed by hidden land mines, abandoned weapons, booby traps, and unexploded ordnance.

Their misery was further magnified by the earlier German flooding of the Pontine marshes outside of Anzio. Near tropical conditions helped turn the again flooded marshes into a deadly mosquito breeding ground. Malaria quickly infected thousands of soldiers and civilians alike, including little Maria.

"I am sorry, *Signora* Forte," intoned the doctor as he removed his stethoscope from Maria's fever-ridden body, "there is little that I can do."

"But you're a doctor," she pleaded tearfully. "There must be something."

"Quinine. Only quinine will work, but I have none to give her."

"What will I do?" she cried.

"I can give you something to help with the fever, but it's not a cure. Just make her as comfortable as possible and pray."

"Pray?"

"Yes, pray. I am afraid that she will die, and I want you to pray that I am wrong."

---

4   From *Man's Search for Meaning* by Viktor Frankl, Copyright © 1959, 1962, 1984, 1992 by Viktor E. Frankl. Reprinted by permission of Beacon Press, Boston.

Maria Civita did indeed pray. The beads slid slowly between her trembling fingers as she knelt beside her daughter's fevered body. *Has it come to this?* Had she somehow survived this contorted war only to have her daughter taken from her by a mosquito? She would climb the steps on Mount Civita a hundred times if that would make this cross go away. Her world was imploding. All that she could do was sit next to a makeshift cot and wait for her daughter to die. Maria Civita was now trapped in a hell more frightening than Dante's worst imagery.

Two weeks had passed, and the fever continued to burn her daughter's motionless body. Day and night, she applied wet compresses to Maria's face and neck, but nothing worked. Late one afternoon, as she reached down to soak one of the folded cloths, she noticed that the water basin was empty. This meant a trip down the hill to the well. It also meant leaving her daughter alone for a few minutes. When she returned from the well, she noticed that Maria was now lying on her side. She had moved! She reached down and touched the child's forehead. It was still warm, but nothing like before. A moment later, Maria's lips moved. The fever had broken. The saint atop the mountain had granted her yet another wish.

In a few weeks, Maria was well enough to resume her chores. While feeding the chickens one day, she glanced down the hill to where a small car had stopped. A man got out, reached into the trunk, and swung a large bag over his shoulder. As the little car sped away, the man began walking up the road toward the farm. Maria ran into the kitchen where her mother and Vittoria were working.

"Mamma, Vittoria," she cried, "there's a stranger coming toward our house. Is it Pappa, do you think?" The women wiped their hands and hurried outside. Vittoria squinted into the morning sun. Suddenly, she was running wildly toward the man, crying, "Angelo, Angelo!"

"It's not Pappa?" pressed Maria.

"No," said Maria Civita, "it's your brother. He's come home from the war at last!"

* * *

Although he had been listed as missing in action, Angelo had, in fact, been captured by the British in North Africa and had spent the duration of the war in a prisoner of war camp in India. Except for Domenico, the family was together at last. Steeled by the ugliness of their wartime experiences, like Pollyanna, they found new hope in the monumental task of rebuilding what was left of their lives. Blessed with an industry acquired from life on the farm, they were able to repair much of the house, replace some animals, and cultivate the land. By 1947, with Italy still under occupational control, Angelo and Vittoria had their second son, Elio.

It was also the year that little Maria climbed aboard the *Marine Falcone* and set sail for the United States, along with Rosario, Attilio, and her mother. She spent most of the crossing leaning over railings as the converted troop ship pitched and heaved through rough seas. It would all be worth it, she mused, for she was about to meet her father. Unlike the rest of the family, she had neither memories nor reference points to connect her with Domenico. She was meeting a man whom she was told was her father for the first time in her young life. As they came down the runway, her mother waved to where her father waited. Maria wondered privately why it had taken so long for this moment to come. She leaned forward and kissed him, but it was a kiss that belonged on a bishop's ring rather than on a father's cheek. She wanted to love him, but like Attilio back on the dirt road to the farm, she wasn't quite sure how.

*   *   *

When the Fortes first arrived in Pittsfield, Massachusetts, they expected life to be different. Their new universe consisted of a tiny four-room flat very near the apartment in which Domenico had lived earlier. While Attilio spent his time flushing toilets and dashing about from room to room switching lights on and off, his eleven-year-old sister, awed by the large piles of snow that lined the roadways, threw herself into them with unbridled joy.

They had expected a language barrier and some cultural differences, but they were not prepared to cope with the weather. It was no longer sunny Italy but rather the dead of a Massachusetts winter that greeted Maria Civita and her children, and they quickly found themselves adjusting to thermal shock.

One day, the shock proved to be much more than thermal. A few weeks after they had settled in, Domenico announced to Maria Civita that he wanted to buy her a new dress, something nice for church. Thrilled by the offer, she agreed with his suggestion that it would also be a good idea if their landlady accompanied them in order to assist in the selection. Next day, the three of them walked the mile and a half to England Brothers Department Store, where she sorted through an array of clothing like nothing that she knew existed. After trying on everything in her size, she finally settled on a simple blue and white floral print and matching purse. *It has been so long,* she mused while rubbing her hand across the smooth fabric. *So many years.* Suddenly, out of the blue, her husband offered to buy yet another dress—this time for the landlady! Stunned, Maria sat quietly as he proceeded with the second purchase. Behind the veneer of silence, however, a fire raged inside. *How could he do such a thing?* Before they had left the store, she vowed that he would learn of the error of his ways.

Domenico was still working on the second shift as a crane hitcher at the General Electric plant. His daily routine included packing lunch for the supper club boys, taking out the garbage, and walking to the nearest bus stand. When he left for work the next day, he noticed the garbage can cover lying on the ground. As he lifted it in order to slide it into place, he suddenly froze. *There, stuffed into the can, was the floral print dress, along with the purse.* He was about to learn that things in America would indeed be different. Maria Civita had declared her own war. She would also be redefining the rules of engagement.

The die was cast. They would not be staying in *that* woman's house one day longer than was necessary. Through some Italian-speaking neighbors, Maria Civita learned of a woman nearby who wanted to sell her house.

"Domenico," she announced, "there is a house for sale on Dewey Avenue. I took Maria with me and learned that the seller's name is Martha Rivlen and that she is asking sixty-five hundred dollars."

"And where are we going to get that kind of money?" he gasped.

"From the bank, like everyone else."

"But I only take home seventy-five dollars a week."

"Don't talk to me. Talk to the bank."

"This is crazy. I tell you, it just can't be done."

It was fitting that the Forte family would spend Independence Day of 1948 moving their meager possessions into their new home at 143–145 Dewey Avenue. It was an unimposing clapboard duplex badly in need of cleaning, curtains, and paint. To Maria Civita, however, it meant six rooms aside and plenty of space in back for a garden. They could live quite comfortably in one half of the house, and rental income from the other side would help nicely with the mortgage. More important, it was theirs, and *she* was gone!

The Forte home at 143–145 Dewey Avenue as it appeared circa 1950. It would serve the family for more than half a century.

* * *

Safely ensconced in their new home, individually and collectively, the family quickly began the task of fitting into their new environment. This meant that both Attilio and Maria would be attending school. Besides the obvious language obstacle, this arrangement posed some unexpected social problems, as they soon found themselves under unwelcome scrutiny. Not only was their austere clothing the subject of criticism, but it was quickly discovered that they were at least two years older than all of the other students—a fact that their classmates would not let them easily forget.

Despite problems such as this, they pressed ahead, determined to settle for nothing less than full acceptance into their new culture. This diligence would soon pay off. In less than three years, Maria had acquired a near-perfect command of English. By her fourteenth birthday, only her family and closest friends knew that she had been in the United States for only three years. For his part, Attilio applied himself well enough that within a year, he was able to enter the same courthouse as his father did in 1935 and take the same oath of United States citizenship. In Maria's case, citizenship was a given. Due to the fact that she had been born in Pico a year after her father was naturalized, she had been an American citizen since birth. As a result, she was the only member of the family to emigrate to the United States under the protection of a U.S. passport.

Recognizing a chance to use his bi-lingual skills, Attilio became the host of a popular Sunday-morning radio program directed toward the now large Italian American community. It was known as the *Italian American Hour*. The project resulted in his acquiring a more-than-passing taste for opera, and he soon found himself participating in actual stage performances. He would appear in operatic casts performing throughout the region for many years. In 1952, he married, and he and his wife presented Domenico and Maria Civita with their first American-born granddaughter.

At twenty-six years of age, his brother Rosario was probably the most disadvantaged of the three siblings. With extremely poor eyesight and too old to take advantage of the educational opportunities available to Attilio and Maria, he had to learn the intricacies of English by stumbling through it on a daily basis. He was, however, able to augment this process through adult education and evening naturalization programs. In spite of this handicap, within two years, he acquired an extensive vocabulary, along with an excellent command of diction. This would prove invaluable within the workplace and in other entrepreneurial pursuits.

Never satisfied, he questioned everything. The same aggressive thinking that enabled him to shepherd the family through the war now drove him to dissect every new challenge and turn it into an opportunity. If the house needed repairs that required an electrician, Rosario would study his every move and, once the job was completed, retrace every line and examine every connection. He even retrieved discarded parts packages so that he could study the schematic diagrams so important for the understanding of electrical circuitry. The same was true of plumbers, carpenters, and telephone repairmen. They came to the house only once and were never summoned again.

Rosario Forte, 1957

*   *   *

Maria Civita continued on her path of long-delayed liberation. Steeled by a history of incessant struggle, she was about to take charge of her own life and, in the process, become a woman of absolutes.

They had been living in the house for just over a year when Maria Civita announced, "Domenico, this kitchen needs new cabinets."

"They look fine to me."

"I have to spend half of my life in this room, and I say they must go!"

"There's nothing wrong with them, I tell you."

"They look like Pico after the war. We need new cabinets."

"Not on my salary we don't."

As in the purchase of the house, the period of negotiation was over. About a week later, Domenico returned home from work to find the kitchen in a shambles. The cabinets had been stripped from the walls, the sink was missing, and the refrigerator waited patiently in the middle of the front room.

"My God, woman," he wailed, "what have you done?"

"I was able to get hold of a carpenter, a nice man. You'll like him."

"But I told you …"

"You never had to boil grass in front of a cave; besides, you'll like it when he's done."

Her new sense of self was not limited to establishing parity in her marriage. Others also felt the sting of her newfound freedom. While the kitchen was in the process of being redone, she asked Attilio to drive her in his car to the lumber company so that she might pick out some molding for the project. He said that he couldn't because he was going on a motorcycle ride with his friends. When the morning in question arrived, she sat quietly in her partially finished kitchen, listening to her son as he prepared to start his motorcycle. She was familiar with the drill. First, he would straddle the bike and push down on the kick-start; then he would twist the handle grips, and the machine would roar into action. *Bram-bram-kaflop-kaflop.* Moments later, a dejected Attilio stood in the kitchen doorway. "Ma," he wailed, "you won't believe this, but someone let the air out of both my tires."

"Oh dear, that's too bad. I guess now you'll be able to take me to the lumber store after all."

Attilio Forte, 1950

With her new kitchen in place, Maria Civita also adopted more creative ways of coping with life's lesser problems. Much to her delight, a new supermarket had just been completed barely a mile from where they lived, and once a week, she religiously shopped there. It was a pleasant experience. The people who worked in the market were always friendly and polite. One or two of them even spoke some Italian. The only problem with this arrangement was the mile-long trek back home, carrying bags full of groceries. Her solution was simple. Since these people were so friendly, they surely wouldn't mind if she borrowed a shopping cart in which to take her groceries home. It made perfect sense. Pleased with this decision, each shopping day, she would wheel her cart out of the parking lot, right past the large sign proclaiming "Attention shoppers: Shopping carts are the property of this store and may not be removed from these premises. Violators will be prosecuted."

Several weeks later, the telephone at the supermarket rang.

"Manager here."

"Hello. My name is Maria Forte, and I am calling for my mother because she can't speak English."

"Hi, Maria. What can I do for you?"

"My mother says she wants you to come by and pick up your shopping carts."

"What shopping carts?"

"The ones in our backyard. There are a half dozen of them, and they all belong to you."

"What?"

"Yes. Every time she shops at your store, she uses one to bring her groceries home."

"Didn't she see our sign?"

"I don't know, but even if she did, she couldn't read it."

An awkward silence suddenly hung in the air.

"I see ... and where can we pick up these carts?"

"At 143–145 Dewey Avenue. My mother says to get them soon because even though they are very nice shopping carts, they are beginning to clutter up our yard."

Maria Civita would continue to *borrow* shopping carts for years, during which time the market would dutifully retrieve them, without prosecution.

*   *   *

Whatever his faults, Domenico had always been a model employee, and when he inquired at General Electric about a job for his son, Rosario was hired on the spot. Shortly thereafter, Rosario married and, along with his wife, moved into the now vacant apartment next to his family. He would become the third Forte to take the oath of citizenship, and within a year, he and his wife had a daughter. She would be their only child.

In mid-summer of 1954, Angelo, who had remained on the farm along with Vittoria and their two sons, sold a small piece of family property and set sail for the United States aboard the *Andrea Doria*. The ship was one of the most luxurious vessels afloat at the time and generally considered to be the queen of the Italian fleet. Clearly, given their meager means, Angelo and his family could not afford the cost of standard passage, so they were assigned a berth in steerage, a section below decks that was set aside for the less fortunate. These accommodations were of little concern to them, because given Domenico's sponsorship, they would soon be united with the rest of their family.

That year also saw the ship *Sardonia* sail into the port of New York carrying Concetta, her husband, and their three sons. The migration was now complete. They settled in Providence, Rhode Island. The following year, Maria, now nineteen, would become the first in the family to graduate from high school, and Attilio and his wife had their second child, a boy.

In 1956, Domenico retired from the GE plant, and his beloved bees and garden again became the center of his world. It quickly became clear, however, that his farming prowess was severely undermined by a serious shortfall in business skills.

"Domenico," Maria Civita would complain, "sometimes I wonder if you can even make change for a dollar."

"What are you talking about?"

"I'm talking about the hard work that you do and then throw away. For months, you tend to your bees and then practically give the honey away. Then there's the garden. All season long, you nurture seedlings, plant crops, water them, fertilize them, cultivate them, weed them, harvest them, and then give them away, too."

"That's not true. I get good money for what I sell."

"Good money? Hah! Take your garlic, for instance."

"What's wrong with my garlic?"

"Nothing. That's the point. They are as big as tennis balls. Do you remember last year when you sold most of your garlic crop to your friend at the Italian market?"

"Yes. I got twenty cents apiece for them," he confidently beamed. "A tidy profit."

"Let's take a closer look at your *tidy profit*. Let's see, you sold three hundred heads of garlic at twenty cents apiece. That comes to sixty dollars total. That doesn't even cover the cost of fertilizer, never mind a *profit*."

"So, I suppose you think you could do better?"

"I already did!"

"You did what?"

"You know the new crop of garlic you hung out to dry a couple of weeks ago?"

"What about it?"

"Yesterday, I trimmed them and brought them down to that nice man who lets me use his shopping carts, and he paid me seventy-five cents apiece for them. That's more than three times what your cheap Italian shopkeeper paid you, and here's the money to prove it." She stabbed defiantly into her apron pocket and placed a handful of wrinkled bills on the kitchen table. "Now," she continued, "let's talk about your honey."

"There's more?" he blinked.

"There is indeed," she added as she placed a jar full of honey next to the bills on the table. "Is this your honey?"

"You know it is," he puffed.

"And how much did you get for it?"

"Fifty cents a jar."

"Well, I want you to know that I just bought this one back from your nice Italian friend for two dollars and seventy-five cents."

Domenico blinked, then blinked again! *Was this the same woman he married?* She had suddenly turned his universe upside down. "I ... I see," he stammered. With this one stroke, Maria Civita had become an equal partner in the family decision-making process that he thought he had controlled for all those years. He also realized that there would be no turning back. He rose slowly from the chair and retreated to his garden. When he had left, she leaned back and sighed, "Yes, life in America is good."

*   *   *

A few days after the discussion of agricultural economics, headlines throughout the world reported an unthinkable disaster at sea. In 1956, just two short years after their son Angelo and his family had arrived in America aboard the *Andrea Doria*, it collided with the Swedish liner *Stockholm* and sank just off the coast of Nantucket. Miraculously, only fifty of the one thousand one hundred and thirty-four passengers and crew would be lost. Twenty-six of those lost were Italian immigrants traveling in C-Deck, which was the main point of impact between the two ships. It was also the same steerage compartment where Angelo and his family had been quartered two years earlier.

A year after the sinking of the luxury liner, twenty-one-year-old Maria married this writer. It would be the first and only marriage by a sibling to someone not of Italian American lineage. The union would produce three children, and by extension, ten grandchildren.

Teenaged little Maria stands in her father's garden. She would be the last surviving member of the Forte family. She died in February 2006, at the age of seventy.

* * *

In 1963, Domenico and Maria Civita celebrated their fiftieth wedding anniversary, and the Americanization of their family continued as Angelo joined his brothers as a naturalized citizen. Always the entrepreneur, he worked for a few years at a local stationery manufacturer and managed to save enough money to purchase a refrigerated truck. Along with his wife and sons, he moved to Jacksonville, where he operated a successful trucking business moving farm produce back and forth between Jacksonville and the Carolinas.

At the time of Angelo's venture, Domenico learned of a statute of limitations that existed under Italian law that restricted the ownership of property by non-residents in Italy. Caught totally unprepared, he rushed to Italy and entered into negotiations with nearby relatives who were interested in purchasing the family farm. Unfortunately, Domenico was no better at selling real estate than he was at selling garlic. Stymied by pressure from a fast-approaching deadline, he was forced to liquidate the property for a mere fraction of its worth; consequently, he recovered barely enough to cover his passage for the return trip home. As this financial disaster was evolving, Angelo's son, Mimino, who was also visiting Pico with his grandfather, became engaged and married a local girl. Domenico, of course, attended the ceremony. It was the first time in nearly half a century that he was present for an important family event.

Meanwhile, back in Florida, Mimino's father, Angelo, was diagnosed with cancer. The doctors there advised him that his condition was terminal. Along with his wife and their youngest son, Elio, he promptly returned to a home on Wachonah Street in Pittsfield in order to obtain a second opinion. It was as grim as the original. One year later, the first of many siblings to have been born to an absentee father would die at the age of fifty. Given a life likely shortened by many years in a prison camp, he elected to spend his final days surrounded by the entire family.

* * *

Accomplishment means different things to different people. Probably the most insightful examples of this may be found in contrasting anecdotes concerning Maria Civita and her son, Rosario. In Maria Civita's case, as she continued to discover her new sense of self, she would derive great personal satisfaction from more simple achievements. As a child, she had been denied schooling, and now, at seventy-one, she was unable to read a billboard, watch a movie, or tell the doctor where it hurt. She was often heard complaining, "In 1910, they thought that sending a girl to school was a waste of time. My name is one of my most important possessions, yet I can't even write it down." This would soon change. She had her daughter Maria write "Maria Forte" on a small recipe card, and using it for a model, she spent many hours at the kitchen table, trying to reproduce it. With pen in hand and tongue curled out of the edge of her mouth, she slowly formed the simple cursive letters. Her initial attempts produced little more than disjointed strings of awkward lettering. Months of patience would eventually prevail, however, and reasonable facsimiles slowly started to form. At last, with success in hand, her first chance to use this new skill would be to write the words "Maria Forte" in her twenty-year-old bankbook. "There," she proudly exclaimed, "it now belongs to me, not some person named X," her mark.

The symbol of her newfound identity.

For his part, Rosario, once wounded in an Allied bombing raid and nearly executed by a German colonel, spent his entire working career at the GE plant. Like the rest of the family, he never forgot the lessons learned on the war-torn farm. Always the problem solver, he spent the rest of his life dissecting, analyzing, and reassembling practically everything that he touched. Besides wiring, plumbing, and carpentry, he acquired self-taught skills in photography and photographic development, television repair, and the final challenge of his life: the collection and repair of rare antique clocks. His success in these matters was made all the more remarkable due to his extremely poor eyesight.

If there was one single event that epitomized Rosario's curiosity-driven talents, it was a job-related event at General Electric. While working as a test man in the GE Distribution Transformer Department, it was his job to test the circuit breakers that were needed to protect the transformers themselves. The task required him to hang a breaker on a chain fall, sink it into a vat of insulating oil, make some electrical connections, and then energize it with a strong jolt of electricity. Inevitably, the breaker would fail to open correctly, so Rosario would make some adjustments to the tripping mechanism and repeat the whole process. It usually took several firings to calibrate the device before it worked as intended. The process had been painstakingly developed by a team of electrical and industrial engineers and had been followed to the letter for many years.

On December 20, 1968, the *General Electric News* announced to the world that an eighteen-year test man named Rosario Forte had just been presented with the largest suggestion award in the history of the department. Undaunted by the rigidity of the existing methodology, Rosario questioned every detail of the testing routine and discovered a way to dramatically increase the efficiency of the breaker testing operation. For this, he was given the (then princely) sum of three thousand four hundred and fifty dollars. Much had changed since he poked though the ashes in the bombed out cornfield.

*   *   *

Domenico and Maria Civita continued on together through their sixtieth wedding anniversary. They had survived decades of separation, years of crisis, and the scourge of two wars. At long last, they had been blessed with a semblance of domestic tranquility. Within a year, however, Domenico died peacefully at home, surrounded by his family. He was eighty-three.

Happier days. Domenico and Maria Civita celebrated their fiftieth wedding anniversary in 1963. They would eventually go on to celebrate their sixtieth.

In 1991, seventeen years after his death, the Italian government
honored Domenico Forte for his military service at Vittorio Veneto.
The award consisted of two decorations and a citation.

* * *

They are almost all gone now. Maria Civita survived her husband by fifteen years; she died in 1989. Rosario followed in 1998 at the age of seventy. Attilio died at seventy-two, in 2004. For the rest of her life, little Maria could not bring herself to read a war story or watch a war movie. With toes forever deformed from wearing the *cioci,* she died on February 23, 2006, exactly fifty-nine years to the day that she first stepped from the gangplank onto the soil at Ellis Island. Of the people living on the farm in Pico, only Vittoria and Mimino are left. They both live in Florida.

Poor, illiterate, and lacking job skills, the family's task in their new country was to build upon the strengths they brought with them, and in doing so, set the standard for their posterity. Thus shaped by their example, third and fourth generation descendants live on after them as successful professionals: dentists, nurses, lawyers, accountants, entrepreneurs, merchants, health care professionals, and educators. When Maria Civita passed away at ninety-three, she spoke very little English and had no idea who George Washington was; nevertheless, she died eternally grateful for the second chance they had been given and proud of what they had done with that chance.

EPILOGUE

On a small rise outside of Pico, the farmhouse still stands. Although Mimino's pig is gone, and Sabetta has long since been properly laid to rest, Vesuvius still sulks in smoldering hibernation, and jars of tomato preserves continue to be unearthed. Here and there, the contours of the land have given birth to new cosmetic vegetation. Decades later, what is left of the church of Saint Antonino sits passively in the middle of the cemetery outside of town, its roofless walls still pocked from battle, its sanctuary still littered with rubble. It stands as a silent monument to the insanity of war.

Partway around the world, on the high ground of St. Joseph's Cemetery in Pittsfield, Massachusetts, there is yet another monument: a rather modest maroon headstone that stands near the edge of the road. It has an engraving of St. Anthony alongside the name Forte. It is barely noticed by most visitors as they gravitate toward the more familiar names of loved ones. Even if one were to stop and study the marker, it wouldn't tell them much; monuments never do. The man and woman buried there are a long way from their starting place in life. The carving identifies them as Domenico and Maria Civita. The war that he fought in is now little more than a collage of scratchy old newsreels. The war that she survived will likely join it someday as a grim shadow in the distant past; wars always do. These people will not be remembered for any grand achievement. They did, however, forever exemplify the malleability of the human spirit. Each had promises to keep. For him, there was the ever-elusive struggle for something better, and for her, a life-long commitment to the integrity of the family. They were born and they died and, in between, bridged challenges that would have destroyed the fabric of most families. Along the way, the essence of their lives may have been severely tested, but it never broke, and it is this legacy that will stand as their most enduring monument.

SUGGESTED READINGS

Atkinson, R. *The Day of Battle: The War in Sicily and Italy. 1943-1944*. New York: Henry Holt and Co., 2007.

Barnett, C. *Hitler's Generals*. New York: Grove Weidenfield, 1989.

Bimberg, E. *The Moroccan Goums: Tribal Warriors in a Modern War*. Westport, CT: Greenwood Press, 1999.

Ellis, J. *Cassino: The Hollow Victory*. New York: McGraw-Hill, 1984

Gander, M. *After These Many Quests.* London: Penguin Books, 1989.

Gilbert, T.M. *The Second World War: A Complete Story.* New York: Henry Holt, 1989.

Lamb, R. *The War in Italy: 1943–1945*. New York: St. Martin's Press, 1993.

Lucioli, M. *I Crimini Degli Alleati: La Campagna d'Italia "43–"45.* www.libreriaeuropa.it.

Marshall Cavendish Corp. *History of World War I and Response 1914-1916.*Tarrytown, NY: Marshall Cavendish Corp, 2002.

Shepperd, G.A. *The Italian Campaign: 1943–1945*. New York: Frederick A. Praeger, 1968.

Sowell, T. *Ethnic America: A History*. New York: Basic Books, 1981.

Starr, C. *From Salerno to the Alps: A History of the Fifth Army*. Washington, DC: Infantry Journal Press, 1948.

Tannebaum, M. *The Fascist Experience*. New York: Basic Books, 1972.

Trevelyan, R. *Rome '44*. Viking Press, New York, 1981.

USAAF. *The United States Air forces in World War II: Combat Chronology of U.S. Army Air Force—May, 1944*. www.usaaf.net/chron/44/may/44.atm.

Von Senger und Etterlin, F. *Neither Fear nor Hope*. New York: E.P. Dutton & Co., 1964.

Zabecki, D.T. *World War II in Europe*. New York: Garland Pub., 1999.

Made in the USA
Lexington, KY
02 July 2010